Power of the Dog

TABLE OF CONTENTS

POWER OF THE DOG
2nd Edition: Fully Updated Expanded

How Dog Beats Man at 37 Feats From Overcoming Depression to Predicting Earthquakes

Les Krantz
and David Aretha

Photos: Courtesy of & licensed from Shutterstock.com

Contributing Writers:
Katherine Don, Tim Knight, Marty Strasen
Book Design: Les Krantz

Cover Design: Les Krantz & Kaitlyn Baer

Prologue

Me, a "Double Vet"

That's me above, Les Krantz, coauthor of this book with David Aretha, my longtime editor and contributing writer to many of my works. The photo is old, but it was not chosen because I want to portray myself as younger or patriotic. It was taken shortly after I enlisted in the U.S. Air Force Reserves during the Vietnam conflict, which is where I got the first inkling to write this book, though it's as much about everyday experiences we and our dogs have, as well as some wartime examples.

During my active duty, the Air Force had me serve and study for six months at a military medical-training facility in Texas to prepare me to be a certified veterinary technician. Military vets and their charges like me maintained the military sentry dogs, which dutifully saved countless lives and limbs in "Nam" and later in the Iraq and Afghanistan wars.

It was in the Air Force that I learned that as smart and well trained as humans might be—and as high-tech as the U.S. Military has become—dogs simply do some things better than man, even highly trained ones with state-of-the-art equipment. Here, we examine the amazing powers of dogs, namely how they outperform man, at home as our pets, as well as at war and at work.

I cannot lay claim to any glory during my six years of military service, which was mainly in Texas and Alaska, but I was privy to various reports and eyewitness accounts of wartime heroics in Southeast Asia. One account stood out in particular.

An Airman whose duty was to patrol a military "flightline"—the runways in the war zone in Vietnam—recounted an unusual night. His dog was displaying vicious behavior as he approached him to go on duty. It was completely uncharacteristic of the loving relationship the two had built, the custom between military sentry dogs and their masters. He snapped, growled, and backed away as he was attempted to be harnessed to go on guard duty with his handler. The dog clearly did not want to go and in fact was so hostile to him that he feared to continue his approach.

The airman, who was clearly puzzled by the dog's actions, told his superiors that it was impossible that he and his dog could patrol the flightline that evening. That night, as it turned out, the Viet Cong staged a raid at the same site at which he and his dog would have been on patrol. They shot at will, set off various explosions, and demolished a guard post.

After hearing of the attack, the airman swore that his dog had been telling him something with his unusual behavior. Had the airman and his dog been on patrol, they would possibly have been killed. He was sure the dog saved his life, not to mention his own furry hide. The next morning, the dog's behavior returned to normal. What happened to whomever took their place is still unknown to me.

There was another incident in Vietnam in which one of the sentry dogs and his handler accidentally fell from an inflatable raft while crossing a lagoon. The GI swam toward shore, sure his dog would follow him, yet the dog swam in the other direction, barking intensely at his handler. It was unusual, he thought, because the dog rarely barked, but he was going crazy, yapping incessantly. The dog hovered around the same spot in the water and did nothing but bark and wail, all the while looking directly at his handler, who was now treading water nearby.

The dog's behavior was so unusual that his handler swam toward him to check things out. Seconds later, in the water where the GI had been earlier, he saw a body in a military flak jacket floating across the stream. He wasn't close enough to identify whether it was friend or foe. Suddenly, the corpse—apparently booby-trapped—exploded as it hit his abandoned raft, right where he had been before the now-obvious warning had been given by his faithful dog. Again, the dog saved his handler, as well as himself.

I'm confident that these accounts and others like them were true, although I am not able to substantiate them after all these years. Thus, I did not include them in the main body of this work, which is a treatise on the amazing, and somewhat mysterious, powers of dogs, which can at times be greater and more effective than man's. I later learned that dogs can do many things better than humans, even when we are aided by the latest technology or a team of experts. This book is about the myriad things that man just cannot beat dogs at, from telepathic and physical feats to the metaphysical and emotional.

Today, decades later, these powers are not nearly as mysterious due to all the research that has been conducted. Researchers of all stripes—animal behaviorists, veterinary researchers, zoologists, medical doctors, and trained psychologists—have been unlocking some of the mysteries of how dogs do the amazing things they do. This is the subject of *Power of the Dog*, which cites their research throughout. It was written decades after I began my lifelong association with dogs, including my stint as a military veterinary technician.

My coauthor and friend Dave and I focus on things at which dog beats man, from saving lives in peril, to predicting the future, to improving the life, health, and wellbeing of the canine's "next of kin," us, the species of man.

Thousands of years ago, we took wolves out of the wild, fed them, pampered them, cared for them, and above all loved them and got their love in return. That wasn't a bad deal for either of us, was it? This book is about both sides of the deal, and it will help you understand dogs and maybe even shed some light on why they understand us, too.

Les Krantz

PART I
A Sixth Sense
Inside Information

Chapter One

Where the Heart Is

Power to Find Its Way Home

No matter how many times we've seen it in movies like Lassie Come Home and Homeward Bound: The Incredible Journey, to name two, it's a scene that never fails to yank the heartstrings. Presumed lost after a lengthy absence, the beloved family dog returns home to the tearful embrace of his stunned owners, who have long since abandoned hope of ever seeing their beloved dog again. As the violins swell on the soundtrack, milking the dog's joyous homecoming for maximum schmaltz, even the most hardened cynics in the audience dab away tears.

Yet these happy endings are not just the stuff of Hollywood fantasy. For it appears that some dogs have a truly uncanny ability to find their way home, often from unfamiliar places, over land and even sea.

Take the wildly implausible but nevertheless documented case of Todd, a Labrador retriever who fell overboard from owner Peter Loizou's yacht in the choppy seas off Great Britain's Isle of Wight in the summer of 2002. Desperate to rescue his pet, Loizou searched these heavily trafficked shipping lanes for Todd, who had seemingly vanished beneath the waves. Four days later, a bereft Loizou steered his forty-foot yacht toward home, convinced that Todd had either drowned or been fatally hit by another boat. Yet in a jaw-dropping twist that Hollywood filmmakers would veto as utterly contrived, Todd not only survived—he swam home. All told, the determined pooch dog-paddled ten miles, battling strong ocean currents that would have exhausted a veteran long-distance swimmer, to reunite with his teary-eyed owner, who rightly called Todd's homecoming an "absolute miracle."

That Todd managed to survive is remarkable in itself, but what makes his story even more astonishing is what he didn't do. When the Labrador retriever went overboard, his master's yacht was approximately a mile off the Isle of Wight. Rather than swim for the nearest shore, however, Todd kept paddling the much greater distance toward his home on the mainland. Once he reached the mainland, Todd paused just long enough to shake the excess saltwater from his coat before resuming his marathon swim in the Beaulieu River, the final leg of his six-hour journey home.

Todd, who obviously could have returned home over a less treacherous land route, is proof, at least to some canine behaviorists, that lost dogs will follow the same path homeward, as they did on the outbound excursion. It's an exercise of memory. This theory could explain the historic case of Bobbie, a Scotch collie-English sheepdog mix. Bobbie was the "poster dog" of canines that find their way home.

In 1923, Bobbie accompanied his owners on a long drive halfway across the American continent, from rural Oregon to Indiana, where Bobbie disappeared after a scuffle with local dogs at a gas station. Although owner G. F. Brazier canvassed the surrounding area and ran ads in the local newspaper, Bobbie remained MIA. After three frustrating weeks, Brazier reluctantly abandoned the search to make the long, sad drive back to his Silverton, Oregon, farm.

Six months later, an emaciated yet exuberant Bobbie reappeared in Silverton, where astonished bystanders watched him bound into the arms of Brazier's youngest daughter, Nova. Somehow, this fanatically devoted dog had made his way across nearly three thousand miles of plains, icy rivers, and mountains to reunite with his owners.

As word of Bobbie's miraculous homecoming spread, details of his six-month journey began to emerge in letters the Braziers received from people who had given Bobbie food and shelter en route. Although he had apparently spent several weeks with a family around Thanksgiving, Bobbie usually just stayed overnight before resuming his travels. More than one letter described him as friendly but anxious, as if he couldn't wait to leave.

Dubbed "the wonder dog" by the press, Bobbie became a worldwide celebrity whose death was marked with a graveside wreath, laid by Hollywood star Rin Tin Tin.

Yet while few dogs have ever been feted quite like Bobbie, his remarkable story is by no means unique. In fact, there have been scores of news stories over the years about dogs presumed lost who materialize, panting and bedraggled, on their surprised owners' doorsteps. One such dog was Freddy, a thirteen-year-old Pekinese who scampered up his Montana owners' driveway a week after being snatched by an eagle and dropped miles from home in a snow-covered forest. Unlike Bobby or Todd, Freddy couldn't fly the same route as his captor the eagle, which begged the question: Do dogs really need to have a previously traveled route "in memory" to find their way home?

Well, there may be a better explanation. Strict empiricists believe that dogs may draw "mental maps" of their environment. Others theorize that dogs probably rely on their keen sense of smell and hearing to navigate in unfamiliar terrain.

But Todd swam home, and water doesn't retain odors, at least not enough for even a dog's sensitive nose to detect. And when Freddy was airborne, could he smell anything as far away as the earth below? Of course not. So how exactly does a dog find its way home?

Cambridge-educated biologist Rupert Sheldrake, whose controversial, unabashedly metaphysical theories on animal behavior polarize his fellow scientists (they've called him everything from a "visionary" to a "crackpot"), hypothesizes that dogs' and other animals' extraordinary homing behavior derives from their access to "morphic fields." If the term "morphic fields" leaves you scratching your head, look to the work of legendary Swiss psychiatrist Carl Jung for clarification. The influential founder of analytical psychology, Jung believed that all of mankind shares memories, psychological traits, and emotions through a "collective unconscious," borne of ancestral experience. Per Jung, we see manifestations of this "collective unconscious" in symbols, dreams, and beliefs that recur in widely differing cultures all over the world.

So think of Sheldrake's "morphic fields" as the equivalent of Jung's "collective unconscious": storehouses of memories and associations, existing outside of time and space, that dogs build up regarding both their home environment and their social group (i.e., owners). Simply put, Sheldrake believes that dogs navigate by tapping into these "morphic fields," which enables them to feel a connection to their home and owners that stretches back and forth in several directions, like an unbreakable elastic band.

Although Sheldrake's Jungian-inspired theory of dogs' homing behavior has raised more than a few skeptics' eyebrows in the scientific community, he does cite compelling, albeit anecdotal evidence for its validity. In the 1930s, German naturalist Bastian Schmidt took a farm dog named Max by van to an unfamiliar location six miles from home. As he followed Max—recording the dog's every move—Schmidt was surprised that his test subject did not rely on his sense of smell to guide him back home. And since Max had never been to the drop site, the dog couldn't look to familiar landmarks to gain his bearings before heading in the direction of the farm.

Sheldrake conducted similar field experiments with a navigationally gifted dog by the name of Pepsi in the 1990s and basically came to the same conclusion. Home seemingly exerted almost a magnetic pull on the dog.

Perhaps the most plausible way that lost dogs find their way home is by engaging in a variety of behaviors, using a number of different techniques just like humans do. After all, when observing dogs, we often use the phrase, "they're so human!" Like man's best friend, we humans, when getting from one place to another, rely on one or more navigational aids: a map, a GPS device, our memories, asking directions, navigating by position of the sun or stars, even on instinct. In sum, when there's a will, there's a way—often many of them—and we do know for sure that a dog's will to be with its master is one of the strongest instincts in all of the animal kingdom.

No matter how lost, how far away, how difficult and arduous the trek, dogs so often, and so miraculously, show up on their masters' doorsteps, panting, squealing with excitement, and just plain thrilled to be back where their heart was all along...at home.

Chapter Two

In the Mood

Power to Sense Our Emotions

Sometimes, it seems, our dogs know us better than our own mothers do. If we're joyous and jubilant, they'll wag their tails. If we're angry and yelling at our kids, they'll run off and hide—or maybe even pee on the family room rug. Dogs comfort us when we're crying, sleep next to us when we're drowsy, and even yawn when we yawn. Dogs might not be able to read our minds per se, but they can read our moods.

Dogs are not the most intelligent creatures in the animal kingdom, but they're among them. Primates (such as humans and chimps) and dolphins have higher IQs, but dogs rate high among the remaining beasts. Certainly, few animals can learn and apply what we "teach" them like dogs do. Border collies, poodles, German shepherds, and golden retrievers are among the quickest learners.

According to Stanley Coren, author of *The Intelligence of Dogs,* canines possess both intrapersonal and interpersonal intelligence. Intrapersonal intelligence is pretty basic: The dog knows not to jump across a ten-foot-wide pothole because she knows she's not going to make it. Dogs' interpersonal intelligence, however, is an elevated kind of "smarts." It means that dogs know how to communicate their intentions to other animals, including humans. The dog that walks to the door and whimpers at you is trying to tell you that he wants to go outside and relieve his bladder. And the pup that looks directly into your eyes and barks demandingly is saying, "Please give me a hunk of that hoagie!" This is interpersonal intelligence.

Even if dogs cannot sense our emotions, they definitely pick up clues about us from our body language. "The ability to read body language, even at a distance, is key to their very survival," asserts Myra Savant, a registered nurse and an expert on dog reproduction. "They must be able to determine when another living entity is friendly and represents no threat to them or their pack, and they need to be able to determine when another living entity is displaying threatening postures. They are very skilled at judging moods because reading 'body language' is key to their survival as a species."

Thus, dogs know how to avoid us. But why do they interact with us? Old-school behaviorists say that dogs only interact with us because we provide them with basic needs—food, shelter, and so on. But a dog's intelligence and feelings for us are more complex than that. Why does your dog sit next to you when you're crying? "Perhaps," quipped Dr. Nicholas Dodman of the Cummings School of Veterinary Medicine, "seeing you in a submissive posture, the dog feels it has to grovel to remain below you in rank. Yeah, right."

No, there's much more to it. Dodman postulates several different ways in which dogs can sense our emotions. For instance, they sense when we are sad. Seemingly every dog owner boasts about how their pup comforts them when they are crying or feeling down. Dogs also sense hostility among those who are quarreling. "Of course," Dodman states, "it can be argued that raised voices might drive the dog away, but I have heard of dogs that sulk even when their owners purposely keep their voices low."

Dogs certainly know when we are happy: When we jump with glee, they do, too—with tails wagging. Dogs may also sense timidity in people. Aggressive dogs are known to take advantage of timid people. They act more aggressively toward them because they sense that they can get away with it—that they can assert more dominance over these cautious individuals. In such cases, dogs are sizing up, or sensing, people's emotions.

Have you ever embraced a loved one in front of a dog? Immediately the pooch reacts, running up to you, pawing you, demanding some attention. Why would the dog care if two humans are putting their bodies together—unless he senses that the people are sharing love, pleasure, or some other wonderful emotion? Dodman believes that the dog senses this—and wants his own lovin'.

After a dog does something "bad," like tearing up the garbage bag or the couch, he often becomes wary of us and acts submissively. Dodman believes that it's not just fear of punishment; instead, the dog senses that we're going to be disappointed in him. "I know dogs that have never been punished and who still act in this way," he asserts.

So far, scientists have not been able to prove that dogs can sense human emotions. (Then again, no one has proved that they can't.) But there is ample anecdotal evidence that they can. Every year, researchers are learning a little more about the psychological dynamics between pups and people.

In 2008, a team of doctors at the University of London made an interesting observation. They discovered that dogs tend to yawn when we yawn. Using a wide variety of breeds, they found that twenty-one out of twenty-nine dogs yawned right after people did the same. Incredibly, the dogs tended *not* to yawn when people just opened their mouths. According to the researchers, the dogs' imitative behavior "may indicate that dogs possess the capacity for a rudimentary form of empathy."

In 2012, Deborah Custance and Jennifer Mayer asserted that dogs are empathic. In their study, the London-based researchers found that dogs routinely tried to comfort people who were crying, even if they were strangers.

Down the road, scientists just might prove what *we* have sensed all along: that dogs love us as much as we love them.

Chapter Three

In Harm's Way

Power to Sense Harm to Its Master

Sara Scott does not know whether or not the postman—if it was, indeed, the postman—meant to do her harm when she was home alone one day as a teenager. Thanks to her dog, she will never know.

"At about noon," she recalls, "the doorbell rang. I managed to drag myself to the door to answer it. My parents had not thought to tell me not to answer the door when I was home alone and it seemed like the normal thing for me to do."

It was a man delivering the mail. No reason for concern, right? Perhaps.

"Are you home alone?" he asked. At this point, Sara began to get worried. Why would he want to know that?

"I didn't know how to answer," she recalls. "In a flash and before I could answer, Cleo came tearing out of our bedroom and got between me and the postman. She was barking so hard and furious that foam was coming from her mouth. It was as though she wasn't even taking a breath in between barks.

"It was aggressive, and you could tell that she meant business. I had never even seen her bare her teeth before. [This time,] she was baring and snapping."

Cleo's display was effective. The postman left. Sara was shaken but unharmed. She, along with her parents upon returning home and hearing the story, was thankful that the family dog sensed something unusual and did something about it.

Sara went on to make a career out of her love for animals. She owns West Coast Pets and helps dogs that have fear or aggression problems when being handled by a groomer or a vet. She will never know how much danger she might have been in years ago. She does know that Cleo was a friend to her that day, and potentially a life-saving one.

Anecdotal evidence does seem to indicate that dogs—many of them, at least—have an innate sense of where and when danger lurks, particularly when it faces their masters. There are countless stories about dogs saving families from house fires, sometimes giving up their own lives in the process of alerting their masters to the danger. This, of course, comes not from any "sixth sense" that dogs might possess but from the use of more concrete senses, especially hearing and smell.

At least two dogs led their handlers down the stairs of the World Trade Center on September 11, 2001, before the buildings came crumbling down as a result of that day's terrorist attacks. This, too, was nothing out of the ordinary. Many dogs are known to be fiercely loyal to their masters and possess the ability to recognize and avoid danger.

"These aren't strange or paranormal events," offers John Caprio, a neurobiologist at Louisiana State University in Baton Rouge, in addressing dogs' ability to recognize not only man-made dangers but natural events like earthquakes and floods. The animals, who are in direct contact with the ground and whose smell and hearing abilities are stronger than those of humans, are reacting to real sensations.

However, other canine reactions are less scientifically
explainable, leading some to speculate that dogs have some innate and difficult-to-understand powers.

A Virginia dog named Harry, for example, began howling uncontrollably while in the care of a vet at the moment his family, on vacation in Florida, had become stranded in a flash flood. There are many stories about dogs that begin howling, yelping, or acting strangely at the moment their masters perish, despite not bearing witness to their final breath. According to reporters who witnessed the event, all three of actor Gary Cooper's dogs began to howl the moment that their master died—even though the dogs were outside his room.

One of the most talked-about examples of animals sensing danger occurred in the aftermath of the 2004 tsunami that claimed thousands of lives in Indonesia and Sri Lanka. There were false reports that no animals were found among the dead. Animal carcasses were, in fact, discovered, but it was no surprise to experts that their numbers were considerably fewer than the thousands of human victims.

"I think animals can sense disaster," H. D. Ratnayake, deputy director of Sri Lanka's Wildlife Department, told Reuters news service after the tragedy seemed to spare most of the animal life at the country's largest wildlife reserve. "They have a sixth sense. They know when things are happening."

Others, however, point to a couple of the traditional five senses when explaining what saves four-legged creatures in such situations.

"Some animals have an acute sense of hearing and smell that allow them to determine something coming towards them long before humans might know something is there," explains Alan Rabinowitz, director for science and exploration at the Wildlife Conservation Society based at the Bronx Zoo in New York.

For dogs in particular, it's impossible to deny the evidence of their protective powers. All the elements for "heroism" are there—loyalty to their masters, keen senses, and the ability to affect positive change with their growls, howls, paws and, when necessary, their bite.

In the summer of 2013, a pair of heroic dog stories captured the world's attention. In Texas, a Chihuahua-poodle mix stepped between a small girl and a venomous rattlesnake. The dog took a bite to the eye in defense of its precious companion. Weeks later, in a scene that was caught on video, a dog in Turkey ran to the seashore to block a toddler from crawling into the water. The event prompted The Huffington Post to run a slideshow of 12 other heroic dog stories.

Family dogs have been known to sense the arrival of their masters. It's not a stretch to say many dogs can sense danger as well, whether or not the physical signs are present. It's a power not easily understood, but a power nonetheless.

"What we're faced with is a lot of anecdotes," says geophysicist Andy Michael of the U.S. Geological Survey in discussing such "powers" among animals. "Animals react to so many things—being hungry, defending their territories, mating, predators...so it's hard to have a controlled study to get that advanced warning signal."

And sometimes, there's no time for an advanced warning signal. Instinct prevails. Just ask Sara Scott, who was happy to have her dog around in a time of need.

PART II
Super Senses
Power Ears, Eyes, & Noses

—Chapter Four—
Big Ears

Power to Hear Faint Noises

It was 4:30 in the morning in Orem, Utah, and Andre Trochez and his wife were fast asleep. At the foot of their bed slept Hercules, a twelve-pound Yorkie-poodle mix. Minutes later, an intruder quietly pried open the condo's screen and sliding doors. The Trochezes snoozed through this quiet invasion. But Hercules, with his superior hearing, bolted to attention.

"As soon as he heard the intruder," Andre told *The Deseret News,* "he went berserk and chased him out of the apartment.... It's really comforting that he knew something was wrong and that he reacted."

Dogs not only can smell and, in some ways, see better than humans, but they also can hear better than people, too. This is one reason why, in the days before alarm systems, canines were often employed as guard dogs. They could hear the footsteps that Ralph the night watchman couldn't. As Hercules the yorkipoo proved, dogs also come in quite handy around the home.

Understanding a dog's hearing requires a simple physics lesson. The first thing to know is that sound frequencies are measured in cycles per second—or hertz (Hz). One hertz equals one sound wave per second. When a great number of sound waves hits our ears each second, we say that the sound has a high frequency. While an exceptionally deep voice can be as low-pitched as 100 Hz, a squealing soprano can reach upwards of 4,000 Hz. The bottom string of a guitar is 165 Hz; the top is 660 Hz. People can hear sounds as low as 60 Hz (thunder in the distance) all the way up to 20,000 Hz—and somewhat higher for small children with brand-new ears. As a point of reference, the highest note on a piccolo is approximately 10,000 Hz.

In the animal kingdom, hearing ranges vary dramatically. A chinchilla would not be a useful "alarm pet" since its hearing range is almost identical to ours: about ninety to 23,000. Fish, birds, and amphibians cannot hear high frequencies. A catfish tops out at 4,000 Hz, a canary 8,000, and a bullfrog just 3,000.

Animals who roam the wilderness—including wolves and their descendants, dogs—have some of the best high-frequency hearing. Scientists believe it's a survival mechanism. Wolves/wild dogs need great hearing to detect prey animals for dinner and to hear which animals might be threatening them. A dog's hearing ranges from sixty-seven to 45,000 Hz, about the same as a rabbit's, raccoon's, and hedgehog's.

While rodents can communicate at very high frequencies, no evidence indicates that a dog can produce this type of communication signal. Nevertheless, a dog can hear rodents' high frequency communication, which helps the canines capture these small prey.

Although the dog's upper frequency limit does not compare to that of a cat (64,000 Hz), mouse (90,000 Hz), or bat (110,000 Hz), it is far greater than a human's. Occasionally, a dog will perk up because it hears a high-frequency sound that our ears cannot detect. Dogs actually experience a whole different world of sound than we do, especially when they're outdoors. We cannot imagine all the noises and smells that waft into their heads. It's no wonder that they are so alert as they trot down the sidewalk.

Dogs also are good selective listeners. Despite the many noises that they hear, they can hone in on those that are important to them. Even if the TV is blaring and the kids are yacking, the dog will hear and react to the distinctive squeaky brakes of "Mommy's" Honda as she pulls into the driveway. Like Hercules, dogs selectively react to noises while they're sleeping. Many dogs will snooze right through their owners' talking, coughing, and kitchen noises, but as soon as they hear a biscuit drop on the floor, they're up in a flash.

Because their hearing is so sensitive, dogs can become disturbed by exceptionally loud noises. Such sounds as vacuum cleaners and lawn mowers can be tumultuous to some dogs. So too can the sound of thunder, which may be one reason why many dogs freak out during a thunderstorm.

Back in the 19th century, Francis Galton (half-cousin of Charles Darwin) invented the dog whistle. For dogs' ears only, this device emits frequencies above 20,000 Hz. A trainer could grab a dog's attention with the whistle while remaining silent to his fellow humans. Modern electronic devices, such as the Dog Silencer Pro, emit ultrasound noises that stop dogs from barking. Manufacturers of these products insist that they do not hurt the dogs' ears.

In addition to hearing high-frequency sounds, dogs can also hear noises that are far away. In the 1960s, zoologist P.W.B. Joslin and his colleagues conducted an informal experiment. When Joslin emitted a howl in Ontario, Canada's Algonquin Park, timber wolves reacted to him four miles away. Humans, however, could not hear his howl if they were more than one mile away. Scientists now believe that dogs' hearing range—meaning distance—is three to four times greater than ours.

Because dogs can hear so well, they're able to help humans who are completely or nearly deaf. Hearing dogs are trained to alert their masters to important household sounds and danger signals, such as the doorbell or a smoke alarm. According to 2012 findings released by the U.K. charity Hearing Dogs for Deaf People, 90 percent of hearing-dog owners said they felt less stressed when with their special canine. Another 85 percent said they were able to cope better with being deaf after being partnered with a hearing dog.

Dogs may be small in stature, but their hearing strength is Herculean—as the yorkipoo from Utah can attest.

Chapter Five

A Different Kind of Vision

Power to See What We Can't

Dogs aren't known for their sharp eyesight, and for good reason: Scientists believe a dog's ability to focus on and clarify a given object (called "accommodation") is only one-fifteenth that of a human's. Yet even in the visual arena, dogs put up a good fight. Their ancestry as nocturnal predators gives dogs powers of vision that humans utterly lack: Dogs can see well in dim light, perceive moving objects from afar, and detect flickering lights.

Archaeologists have unearthed evidence that this unique sense of sight was the reason dogs were first welcomed into towns and cities. The very first civilizations were in the Middle East and Northern Africa. Etchings and rock paintings from this era repeatedly depict dog-like animals that are akin to modern sighthounds. The pictures show these dogs on a leash, being led into the hunt.

The dual dog ability to detect motion and see well in dim light was exactly what ancient humans needed. The earliest civilizations arose in a desert landscape, so the ability to detect motion over long distances would have been vital in hunting. Humans could shoot game from far off because they had bows and arrows, but they couldn't detect the game over open desert expanses. This is why hunting dogs were used. Humans also can't see well at night, so they were unable to defend their burgeoning cities from intruders. This is why watchdogs were introduced to civilization.

So while dogs have an amazing sense of smell, it was actually their vision that made them useful to ancient peoples. Scientists believe sighthounds were the first dog domesticates of Africa and Eurasia, making modern sighthounds some of the most ancient dog breeds. Ancient sighthounds were treated like gods, and even in modern times, sighthounds are venerated in Middle Eastern and Northern African cultures. In both Bedouin and Egyptian languages, salukis (an ancient sight-hound breed) are called "the noble ones," and they are exempt from the Islamic law that asserts that dogs are unclean.

In 1875, a famous westerner witnessed first-hand the mysterious reverence with which sighthounds are treated. Lady Anne Blunt, Lord Bryon's granddaughter, was traveling through the deserts of Arabia, guided by nomadic Bedouin tribespeople. The Bedouin were very fond of a dog they called the saluki, which Lady Anne mistook for a greyhound. On three separate occasions, Bedouin guides gave Lady Anne a sighthound as a gift. They considered this the ultimate demonstration of hospitality.

As Lady Anne traversed the deserts of Jordan, her guide brought along his favorite dog, which he called Sayad, meaning "hunter." Sayad was responsible for killing the desert hares, birds, and hyenas that sustained the humans during their long desert journey. Lady Anne reported in her journal that Sayad was a "very handsome greyhound...of the long-haired breed, which has a wonderful nose for game. His master declares he sees the birds, for the Arabs do not seem to understand the theory of scent."

Lady Anne was mistaken. While British biologists had already discovered the dog's unequaled sense of smell, sight-hounds don't use their noses when they perceive hares darting across a desert landscape, hundreds of feet away. They are taking advantage of their acute sensitivity to movement, which is made possible by the special architecture of the canine eye.

Dogs, like the wolves they evolved from, have eyes that enable them to hunt during the night. Dog pupils are large, to let in as much light as possible. Once an image has entered through the eye's pupil, it passes through the lens, which in turn focuses the image onto the retina, which is located along the back wall of the eyeball.

It is the anatomy of the retina that limits a dog's visual acuity, while simultaneously allowing the dog to detect movement in dim light. The retina is lined with cells that are light-sensitive, called photoreceptors. The eye of any mammal has two main types of photoreceptor cells: rods and cones. Rods are especially sensitive to light, and are also associated with perception of movement.

Cones, meanwhile, are the receptors of fine detail and visual acuity. Most mammals have both rods and cones in their retinas; dogs tend to have a higher proportion of rods. The central area of the retina in the canine eye contains about 20 percent cones, while humans have an area called the fovea that consists of 100 percent cones.

To make their night vision even better, dogs have an extra layer of cells called the "tapetum lucidum," located directly behind the rods and cones of the retina. When light that gets past these rods and cones hits these cells, they reflect the light almost straight back out. This means a dog has two chances to perceive light: When the light is reflected, it has a second chance to be absorbed by the photoreceptors. The tapetum lucidum is responsible for that shiny look in dogs' eyes when you shine a light in them at night.

Once again, these forces that improve a dog's night vision also lower visual acuity. Paul Miller, a research professor of comparative ophthalmology at University of Wisconsin, Madison, says that "although the tapetum improves vision in dim light, it also scatters some light, degrading the dog's vision from the 20:20 that you and I normally see to about 20:80."

So while our canine cousins excel in night vision and perception of movement, they have poor acuity. From a dog's-eye view, there is little need to perceive the details of nearby, stationary objects. Dogs are evolved from canids (a family that includes wolves, foxes, jackals, and coyotes), which hunted over large tracts of land. For them, the ability to detect movement over distance was more important than seeing nearby objects. A dog has its sense of smell for this type of fine distinction. Humans evolved from rainforest primates who never saw over open distances (there were too many trees in the way), yet they needed to use detailed visual cues (mostly color) to determine which of the rainforest's many fruits, vegetables, and nuts were poisonous or not.

Dogs are not good at seeing details. Many owners have realized that their own dog is not good at recognizing them until they speak out loud. Dog breeder Caroline Coile recounts with amusement her dogs' apparent inability to recognize her by sight: "The dogs sniff the air, crane their necks, stare, and begin to pace and bark nervously. It is apparent they're not sure who I am.... I finally speak, and the relief is palpable as they swamp me with enthusiastic greetings. The scary part is, these are salukis—sighthounds!"

Also, dogs don't distinguish colors as well as humans. They see only variations of blue, yellow, and brown, along with black, white, and gray. However, Russian researchers discovered in 2013 that dogs are not as "color blind" as once thought. Previously, scientists thought that the dogs discriminated between objects by the items' darkness or brightness. But the Russian researchers learned that their test dogs were much more likely to recognize a piece of paper by its color than its brightness level.

The propensity of rods in a dog's eyes has another curious side effect—dogs are extremely sensitive to flickering light. The light frequency at which flickering lights appear to fuse into a constant image is called "flicker fusion," and it differs from one species to the next. Dogs have high flicker fusion. The benefit of this is unknown, but it does cause trouble for those dogs that spend hours barking at the tantalizing play of light and shadow on the wall. This also means dogs probably don't enjoy watching television, as to them the image is rapidly flickering, rather than the smooth image that humans perceive.

Dogs, then, wouldn't have the visual acuity to pass even the most forgiving driver's license test, and they don't recognize details of an object held in front of their very eyes, unless they can smell it. But this apparent blindness is not too much of a price to pay for the other powers of vision that a dog boasts—the ones that allow dogs to stand guard, peering out into the night, ready to alert their master to the slightest of movements.

—Chapter Six—
Real Smellers

Power to Smell 50 to 100,000 Times Better than Humans

Dog owners know the routine. "Go potty. C'mon, go potty." Dogs all too frequently seem much more interested in sniffing every square inch of grass than getting down to business when you need them to.

A dog is not just sniffing. He is experiencing the world in a way only dogs can. And considering what a dog is experiencing through his keen sense of smell, perhaps humans ought to be thankful that they are not able to experience the world in this way.

What, exactly, is a dog's powerful nose picking up? The scents of various neighbor dogs and their own "lawn watering" trails. The pudding remnants spilled last Tuesday by the toddler next door. Even the small patch of dried blood on a week-old bandage.

"While people tend to describe the world as what we can see, your dog's description is based on a keen sense of smell," contends Ed Presnall, a longtime dog trainer and an authority on dog tracking.

The reason dogs possess this power is physiological. Within their two nostrils are anywhere from 125 million to 300 million receptor cells, depending on the breed, that can detect scent. Humans possess about 5 million. The moisture from dogs' typically cold, wet noses captures and dissolves molecules and brings them into contact with a superior olfactory epithelium—the area of the nasal cavity on which the receptor cells are found.

"Another way to look at the size difference," Presnall points out, "is the dog's epithelium is roughly the size of an 8 ½-by-11 page, while the human's is about the size of a postage stamp."

Dogs tend to be active sniffers, as most owners can attest. Their sniffing occurs through a rapid series of short inhales and exhales that differs drastically from the normal breathing pattern. The odor molecules picked up, if not recognizable to the dog in a single sniff, can actually be accumulated over a series of sniffs until recognition occurs. Nerve impulses are transmitted from the receptors to the dog's brain, which has a highly developed olfactory "bulb" capable of distinguishing millions of scents. It's no wonder that certain dog breeds specialize in tracking, inspecting, and identification. More commonly, dogs can be found sniffing—well, how shall we say—certain private areas on other dogs.

While owners are often embarrassed by this, or consider the behavior reprehensible, this nasal curiosity serves a multifaceted purpose for dogs. Evidence suggests that dogs identify one another this way, perhaps from the anal sacs that secrete chemicals that bear a "signature odor" for each dog. Dogs can also determine the sex and sexual receptivity of another dog by sniffing urine and feces. Some dogs can even identify their own relatives through scent.

Until an accurate method of measuring a dog's smelling power is invented, no one can know for sure just how much stronger dogs pick up scents than humans. Estimates range from fifty times better to 100,000 times better.

Dogs' noses are so powerful, in fact, that at times their overwhelming sense of smell can seem debilitating.

Janice Biniok was scheduled to demonstrate at a large pet expo with her dog, Blazer—a pooch that had performed on many occasions before large crowds, in loud settings, and even with other dogs sniffing his rear end. At this particular expo, Blazer did something he had never done before. He refused to perform at all. Biniok was perplexed. After her initial embarrassment and disgust over Blazer's apparent disobedience, she realized what the problem had been: bird poop.

"A parrot demonstration on the stage immediately before our performance had left bird poop on the stage," she recalls, "and the new scent was so overwhelming for the dog that he just couldn't concentrate on anything else. He absolutely couldn't ignore it like he could ignore so many other types of distractions.

"That experience made me realize what a strong impact scent has on canine behavior. Sometimes, when we think our dogs are misbehaving, they're just 'seeing' something we can't see."

Humans may never fully understand the powers dogs possess in their wet little noses, but it will not stop them from putting those powers to use. A Labrador named Villain, an arson-detection dog just outside Tampa, Florida, routinely uses her nose to uncover evidence.

"You're looking for a needle in a haystack," offers her trainer and handler, Bill Whitstine. "The dog sniffs and then points to an object with a trace of accelerant on it, say something in parts per billion.

"With a mechanical sniffer, even if it were equal to a dog, and it is not, I'd still have to point it at just the right spot to make it register. The dog does the pointing, and I just have to take the sample."

Chapter Seven

Directional Hearing

Power to Locate the Source of Sounds

Fergus lies in slumber on the deck, sleeping through all the chatter of the backyard barbeque. Nothing, it seems, will wake him from his slumber until—*crack*—a twig snaps in the bushes. Fergus bolts to attention. An enemy rodent is trying to enter the yard, but where exactly is it? The crackling continues, and Fergus tries to hone in. He twitches his pointy ears, turns his head back and forth, and then tips his head on an angle. With his elaborate hearing system, Fergus has detected with pinpoint precision the location of his adversary: third bush from the garage! He charges in that direction, assured of victory.

Though dogs enjoy their comfy lives as domesticated pets, they were born to be wild—or at least their ancestors were. Living in the wilderness, they developed a heightened sense of

42

hearing (as well as smelling and eyesight) in order to survive and thrive. Dogs needed exceptional hearing so that they could hunt for food, avoid being another animal's lunch, and protect their young as well as the other members of their pack.

In general, predators—including the carnivorous canines—are better at locating sounds than other animals. When on the hunt, the wild dogs of yore could hear a distant flitter in the grass or a crunch in the brush. It could have been a bunny for breakfast or a squirrel for supper. While living in the wilderness, dogs kept their ears open for animal noises—even while sleeping. After all, some ferocious beast might have posed a threat to themselves and their pack members. The dogs needed to be aware of noises at all times.

Even today, as domesticated animals, dogs are on high alert. They react to any out-of-the-ordinary noise that they hear outside, be it a voice, crackle, siren, or animal call. Just imagine how a Yorkie would react if he heard a lion's roar for the first time.

Like other animals, including humans, dogs detect the direction of a sound with their two-ear system. Say Rufus, a blind dog, is attending a baseball game and sits in a box seat behind first base. When the batter hits the ball, Rufus knows that the sound came from the left because his left hear heard a stronger sound; his skull had walled off the sound waves from his right ear. According to Stanley Coren in *How Dogs Think,* a dog also would know that a sound came from the left because the noise reached the left ear faster. Coren asserts that a dog "can distinguish differences in the arrival time of sounds by as little as...one eighteen-thousandth of a second!"

Some dogs have better directional hearing than others. It has been postulated, although not proven, that dogs with pricked ears—those that stick up—have the best ability to localize and detect sounds. Huskies, collies, shepherds, and terriers all have pricked ears. Other breeds have semipricked ears, while many others—like poodles and bloodhounds—have floppy ears.

A dog's outer ear (pinnae) includes a large number of small muscles, allowing the dog to raise, tilt, and rotate its ears. It is almost like the dogs have their own radar system; they can hear sounds all around them and precisely determine where the noise came from.

Though our ears are not as sophisticated as dogs', we are also good at detecting the location of a sound. But where dogs outdo us is when the sound is faint. Dogs' ears are much more sensitive to noises than ours; they can hear things that we can't. For example, veterinarian Laura Hungerford points out, "a dog could hear a siren farther away than we could."

If a person gets lost in the woods, it makes sense to bring the family dog on the rescue mission. Not only would the dog be the first to hear the person's cry for help, but it has the ability to lead you in that direction.

—Chapter Eight—
I Know That Smell...

Power to Make Identifications by Smell

On a sunny Christmas afternoon in 2007, veterinarian Eric Lei was hanging out on the first floor of his house in Sai Kung, China. Dr. Lei is by no means a man ignorant to a dog's keen sense of smell, but what was about to happen took even this veteran veterinarian by surprise.

Dr. Lei's four dogs, along with his cats, were several stories above, sunbathing on the roof. Several stories below, Dr. Lei opened a bag of potato chips. He was peacefully munching on this innocent afternoon snack when, as Dr. Lei recounts in the *South China Morning Post,* "there was a loud clamoring of lots of little feet rushing down the stairs like a mini-stampede...and four drooling dogs suddenly surrounded me with desperate looks in their eyes." Dr. Lei's knowledge of dog physiology immediately led him to the conclusion that the dogs had sniffed the chips, all the way from the rooftop.

The incident was particularly surprising given the breeds of Dr. Lei's dogs. Three of the dogs were toy breeds—definitely not known for their sense of smell. The fourth was an Afghan hound, a sighthound bred for acute vision rather than smell. There *are* dogs bred to have discriminating senses of smell. They are known as scent hounds, and they include the bloodhound, beagle, and basset hound. Even Dr. Lei's toy breeds—among the last dogs to be picked in the great game of scent identification—display a sense of smell that would put any human nose to shame.

A dog's ability to differentiate between scents could legitimately be considered the crème-de-la-crème of dog superpowers. Other abilities, like sniffing out drugs, detecting cancerous cells, and even predicting oncoming natural disasters, all relate to this refined sense of smell. As we humans navigate the world through sight, a dog's world is almost entirely organized by scent.

Dogs don't merely have a *strong* sense of smell; they have an unbelievably *discriminating* sense of smell. Just like humans, dogs smell something when itty-bitty molecules, called "odorants," emit from nearby objects. These odorants release energy when they come into contact with the olfactory epithelium, located in the nose. The odorants then bind with "olfactory receptors," and from there nerves shoot off messages to the part of the brain that deals with recognizing smell (the olfactory bulb). The brain recognizes the particular smell only if it has already been categorized into the animal's long-term "smell memory." If the smell is not recognized, the brain creates a new memory.

The number of individual smells that an animal can recognize and store away depends on the quality of the given species' olfactory equipment. At each stage of the smelling process, a dog's capabilities are superior. Humans have 5 million receptor cells in the olfactory epithelium; some dog breeds have roughly 200 million. Dogs also commit a larger proportion of their brains to smell-identifying tasks. Since different olfactory receptors specialize in identifying different smells, a dog brain can perceive far more distinct odors than a human brain can.

The best way to understand a dog's sense of smell is to compare it to people's sense of sight. Explains professional dog trainer Ed Presnall, "We see in color while our dogs smell in color. Humans have the ability to differentiate between approximately 16 million colors...and distinguish about one thousand individual smells, while dogs can easily identify 1 million or more individual scent patterns."

Presnall adds: "I like to say that if you took your dog into a bakery, you could smell the bread, yeast, and chocolate while your dog could identify the dozens of individual ingredients in each pastry, loaf of bread, or cake."

It seems that dogs rely almost entirely on scent in their perception and categorization of the world. The extent of this was shown in a 2002 study conducted by Irit Gazit and Joseph

Terkel at Tel-Aviv University. The researchers tested six dogs that had been trained to identify the smell of explosive materials. In a controlled test environment, the dogs looked for the explosives in conditions both dark and light. The intention was to find out how much dogs relied on smell versus vision in tracking the explosives. Prior to the experiment, the dogs were taught what the explosives smelled *and* looked like. The researchers were already aware that dogs relied *mostly* on their noses, but the results were striking.

A dog's ability to see had absolutely no effect on its ability to find the explosives. As the researchers note, "even when the container was clearly visible from the position where the dog was standing, rather than approach it directly the animal would continue to search in a typical olfactory search pattern."

Humans have little trouble finding practical applications for this dog power. Dogs have been used to find anything from dead bodies to illegal currency to smuggled agricultural products. Cattle ranchers have learned that dogs can even smell when a cow is in estrus (receptive to mating). So the next time a dog seems rude in sniffing out a stranger, keep in mind that, just as we remember people not by name but by face, a dog won't know who you are until it gets a good whiff.

PART III
Soothsayers and Crystal Balls
The Ability to Predict the Future

Chapter Nine

A Storm's A-Brewin'

Power to Detect Thunderstorms

In Florida, meteorologists make six-figure salaries and news organizations spend untold millions to predict the weather. After all, tropical storms can devastate the Sunshine State in a matter of minutes. Sometimes, a storm can slam a town without much of a warning. That's why the Mastrogiovanni family takes pride in its four-legged weatherpup: Sydney.

Normally, Sydney is a happy-go-lucky dog who loves to play. However, her demeanor becomes more serious when she senses a change in the weather. Sydney stops in her tracks and begins to sniff the air. "It took a little while for us to figure out what she was doing," Mike Mastrogiovanni says. "But then we put two and two together and realized, okay, she's putting her nose in the air and here comes a thunderstorm.

Usually about ten to fifteen minutes before the storm is noticeably present, [we'd] be able to tell there's a storm coming because of her actions."

In today's world, we do not place much value in dogs' weather-predicting ability. After all, the Weather Channel and various Internet sites can also give us up-to-the-minute forecasts. But imagine how helpful dogs were generations ago, prior to television and radio. When the family dog started to sniff, circle, bark, whimper, or howl, rural families figured that maybe it was time to go inside—and perhaps board up the windows.

Traditionally, people have credited dogs and other animals with having a "sixth sense" for predicting weather changes. "It's long been talked about in folklore," says Florida meteorologist Randy Rauch. "You'll hear all kinds of stories that dogs, cats, cows, crickets—all have some sort of knowing power before severe weather." But the idea of a *sixth sense* is hogwash. States Mary Burch, a certified applied animal behaviorist: "Dogs don't have a sixth sense as much as they do five keen, extraordinary senses that are more highly tuned than the senses of humans."

Even if their humans are clueless about an upcoming storm, dogs have the ability to feel it, smell it, hear it, and see it.

Feelin' it: Although rises and drops in barometric pressure affects humans' bodies, we typically are not aware of the changes. Many animals, though, do take notice. When the barometric pressure drops, and therefore conditions become ripe for a storm, birds respond by flying away from the bad weather. Dogs also might be sensitive to a drop in barometric pressure—much more so than humans. With experience, many dogs learn to associate this feeling with an upcoming storm. Scientists also believe that animals can detect electrical changes in the air; i.e., lightning.

Smellin' it: Dogs might also smell a storm, which explains why Sydney stops to sniff when a storm is brewing. Lightning ionizes the air, forming ozone—which has a distinctive metallic smell. Even when the lightning is miles away and unnoticeable to humans, dogs still might be able to smell its effects. Burch points out: "Dogs have the remarkable ability to smell cancers and the scent a prison escapee has left on keys that have been dropped into a rapidly moving creek. So it's no surprise that they smell a hurricane or rainstorm coming before we think about reaching for an umbrella."

Hearin' it: Dogs not only hear high-pitched sounds better than humans; they can also hear low-pitched sounds very well, including the groan of distant thunder. When a dog hears the rumble, he associates it with an upcoming storm.

Seein' it: Same thing here. When dogs see the skies darkening and clouds forming, they associate the changes with storms of the past. It is unclear whether dogs can see these changes better than humans can. However, one study indicated that dogs are able to differentiate between subtle shades of gray better than us, so perhaps they are exceptional at identifying storm clouds.

Dogs who *fear* thunderstorms are likely to be more attuned to all of these atmospheric changes. A crack of lightning and a rumble of thunder causes many dogs to panic. They feel that something is terribly wrong—that something they're not used to is happening. They pant, howl, whimper, bark, pace, circle, and/or relieve themselves in a place where they shouldn't. Some dogs cuddle next to their favorite person and start to tremble. Other dogs become destructive and take out their angst on the throw pillows.

Early in the book/film *Winn Dixie,* the title character goes on a barking fit in Opal's and her father's trailer home during a storm. Later in the movie, Winn Dixie runs away during a downpour. Recalls Chris Walkowicz, author of *Choosing a Dog for Dummies,* "I've had others lie in the bathtub or wrap themselves around the toilet stool, grounding themselves. One German shepherd was so terrified, he tore apart a chain link fence, severing the main artery under his tongue."

Animal behavioral specialists offer numerous tips to keep your dog calm during a storm. You should stay calm, brush or pet her, and offer soothing words. You could distract her by tossing a ball, and you could muffle the storm's noise by closing windows, turning on a fan, or playing loud music. You could even create a dark, safe place for your dog (her own shelter). You and your loved ones should also remain calm. If you freak out and go "Whoa!" whenever thunder crackles, it would make your dog even more agitated.

For storm-fearing canines, you can use your dog's premonitions to his advantage. In other words, once *you* sense that *he* senses that a storm is looming, you can immediately commence Operation Tranquility: Pull the shades, turn on the fans, and calm him down. You can thus create a comforting doggy haven before the storm even arrives. Perhaps, if we dare to speculate, that was his intention all along.

Chapter Ten

The Final Goodbye

Power to Sense Impending Death

In *How Dogs Think,* author Stanley Coren recalls the ominous words of Aunt Lila, an old woman whom he had met in Kentucky. If a dog emitted two howls close together, she warned, it meant that a man was about to die. Three howls, she insisted, meant that a woman was about to meet her maker.

God help you, Lila implied, if you made eye contact with a dog before it delivered multiple howls. Because, Lila says, "dogs look in the direction of the person about to die."

Before you write off Aunt Lila's words as folklore, or just plain nonsense, consider the story of Scamp the schnauzer. In The Pines nursing home in Canton, Ohio, Scamp patrols the halls like a pint-sized Grim Reaper. Guests find the white and gray-haired dog adorable, but residents become gravely nervous when the schnauzer starts paying them too much attention. Scamp, it seems, can predict who is about to die.

In the summer of 2007, Scamp's morbid premonitions drew international attention. Over the previous three years, he had "predicted" nearly every one of the nursing home's forty deaths. "He has either barked or he'll pace around the room," says Deirdre Huth, a staff member at The Pines as well as Scamp's owner. "The only time he barks is when he's trying to tell us something's wrong."

One day, Yvette Notturno received a dreaded call. It seemed that Scamp wouldn't leave the side of her close friend, Andrew Popa. Notturno rushed to the nursing home, and Popa died shortly after.

Scamp himself had a near-death experience as a puppy. Hit by a car, his pelvis was crushed and his colon punctured. It took him six weeks to recover. He went on to live a purposeful life. Employee Adeline Baker says Scamp was "very sensitive to the families and the needs of the residents. He knows when someone is not doing well—he'll camp out in their room."

Scamp isn't the only dog that can sense death in human beings. Anecdotal evidence abounds. Legend has it that when Britain's Lord Carnarvon died while in Egypt in 1923, his dog, Susie, howled back in England—then dropped dead herself. In more modern times, Hazel O'Neill of Scotland recalls bringing her dog to a care home. After bedtime for the residents, O'Neill and a coworker were enjoying tea when her dog started pacing between O'Neill and a patient's room. "After the second time he came back, we followed him to the room only to discover the resident had died following a massive heart attack," O'Neill recounts. "I am convinced that animals are able to sense death."

Few scientists have explored this phenomenon, although several theories have been proposed. Some say simply that dogs are good at detecting emotional changes in their owners. For example, they often come up to us when we hurt ourselves or when we are crying. Similarly, the theory goes, dogs will appear upset if their (dying) owner is inactive, depressed, and not herself. Writes Mary Burch: "When people are dying, they stop moving around, they speak with a voice that is much weaker, and they may appear wobbly or frail. All of these dying behaviors are easily observed by dogs."

One theory starts with the premise that dogs, who descended from wolves, are pack animals and that the wellbeing of the other pack members is critically important to them. As such, dogs developed a heightened sense of awareness of pack members being sick—or dying. Because domesticated dogs consider their human household companions as pack members, they can instinctively determine when they are ill or about to die.

According to another theory, dogs sense a change in chemicals in a dying human's body. Studies have already shown that dogs react to their owners' cancer cells. Dogs have scented cancers in lungs, breasts, bladders, and other parts of the body before conventional diagnosis.

Since a person's body chemicals change before they die—including a breakdown of enzymatic activity—perhaps a dog detects the difference.

Dogs seem to sense not only others' death but their own death too. There are thousands of examples, if not millions, of dogs wandering off to die. In many cases, they have "said their good-byes" to the members of the household, perhaps by licking their faces, before departing. Since we cannot conduct postdeath interviews with dogs, it is impossible to know for sure why they do this. Some dog owners believe that the kindly canines don't want their masters to suffer the pain of watching them die. Veterinarians have speculated that the dying dogs are afraid and they don't want their owners to see their fear. We do know that this not just a dog phenomenon. Many cats, elephants, horses, and other animals also wander off to die.

"Typically, when animals are dying, they don't feel well," Burch writes. "They may be in some pain, or they may be aware their bodies are shutting down. Taking yourself to a corner of the yard will allow you to lay down in peace where no one will disturb you." Burch added: "Going off to a quiet place would also be a good protective move based on evolution. If you are no longer in a position to fight off predators because you are sick and weak, going to a quiet corner will keep you out of the way of any trouble that comes along."

Sometimes, it seems, dogs have a morbid preoccupation with death. Stories have circulated about dogs wandering around to look for a recently deceased loved one and finally stopping when they reach his or her grave. In Edinburgh, Scotland, in 1858, a dog named Greyfriar's Bobby found the grave of his recently deceased owner, John Gray. And once he found it, he never left, keeping vigil at the burial spot for fourteen years until he himself breathed his last breath. It was the ultimate example of loyalty to the death.

Chapter Eleven

What's Shakin'?

Power to Predict Earthquakes

In summer 2002, the Alaska Earthquake Information Center welcomed a new employee named Josh Stachnik—but perhaps they should have hired his dog instead. That October, during his very first day with his new owner, Fats proved he had special powers.

When Stachnik, twenty-five, went to bed that night,

Fats—a chubby Rottweiler/Chesapeake Bay retriever with one bad eye—slept on the floor next to his owner's loft. But at 3 a.m., Fats began to whine. Josh woke up. Was his new dog having trouble adjusting to his new home...or was it something more serious? Fats began pacing around the cabin, very distraught. Stachnik got up, and after a while he heard his stove creaking and saw his loft sway back and forth. Oh God, Stachnik realized, Fats had sensed an earthquake.

Then, on the afternoon of November 3, Josh drove along the Denali Highway with his friends, Kelly Kore and Bart MacCormack—as well as his faithful companion. Fats had been out of sorts all morning, barking excessively and sniffing the ground. Recalls Kore in *Alaska Science Forum,* "I jokingly said to Josh and Bart that maybe we were going to have another earthquake." At 1:12 p.m., Stachnik's Ford Excursion began to shake violently, even after he put it in park. Josh and his friends braced themselves and waited out the Denali Earthquake, which at 7.9 was the most violent quake in the world in 2002. Within weeks, Fats had sensed the coming of not one but two earthquakes. But he was hardly the first dog or animal to notify humans of upcoming rumbles. Stories of animals "predicting" earthquakes date back more than two thousand years.

In 373 B.C., days before a giant quake devastated the Greek city of Helice, such creatures as rats, snakes, and weasels evacuated the area. Often, canines are the ones who give off warning signals. In 1995 public health workers in Japan recorded accounts of excessive dog barking just prior to the Kobe earthquake, which claimed six thousand lives. In 2001, many people in the Seattle area claimed that their dogs had barked frantically prior to an earthquake.

In 2004, days before the infamous Asian tsunami (under-ocean earthquake) that killed tens of thousands of people, animals in the region began acting oddly. Elephants screamed and ran for higher ground, and dogs refused to go for walks on the beach or even leave the house. Ravi Corea of Sri Lanka says that just prior to the tsunami, his friend could not get his two dogs to jog with him on the beach. "They are usually excited to go on this outing," Corea says. But on that fateful day the dogs refused, which probably saved their owner's life.

In 2013, in the Sichuan province of China, authorities put earthquake predictions in the paws of pooches. A month after two hundred residents were killed or unaccounted for following a quake, the earthquake authority of Nanchang announced it would keep dogs on active duty because they "act abnormally when an earthquake is coming," sometimes up to ten days in advance, an official said.

Many people have claimed that certain creatures have a "sixth sense," a special kind of power for sensing the future. But scientists offer several more legitimate reasons that explain why dogs and other animals can "predict" earthquakes. The first relates to their keen sense of hearing. Many animals, including dogs, are better than humans at hearing sounds with low frequencies. It is possible that the animals heard a strange "rumble" in the distance. Elephants have exceptional low-frequency hearing, which may explain why they were among the first animals to act hysterically before the tsunami.

Many scientists believe that animals can feel

the ground's subtle vibrations before the full-fledged earthquake. All mammals, including people, have highly sensitive sensors called Pacinian corpuscles in their feet and joints. Humans, however, have become out of touch with this sense of touch. "Animals are always in direct contact with the ground," explains Joel Greenspan, a sensory neuroscientist at the University of Maryland-Baltimore. "We don't do that anymore. We have shoes and clothes. We pay attention to other people, sights, and sounds." The Pacinian corpuscles theory may explain why Fats was barking and sniffing the ground on the morning of the Alaskan earthquake.

Scientists have posited other explanations for animals' "earthquake premonitions." They believe that animals detect electrical changes in the air and/or gas released from the earth. Dr. Helmut Tributsch explains that when quartz rock (which comprises much of the earth's crust) is pressured in a certain way, positive and negative ions can shift slightly. This produces an electrical charge. According to Tributsch, the piezoelectric effect of the quartz is capable of generating enough electrical energy to create airborne ions before and during an earthquake. This electrostatic charging of aerosol particles may be what dogs and other animals react to.

Some humans, and perhaps some animals, experience persistent headaches for days prior to earthquakes. Some scientists have attributed this to changes in the earth's electromagnetic field. Geologist Jim Berkland said that a dog was observed chewing on willow bark—from which aspirin is derived—prior to an earthquake. Dr.

Berkland believed that the dog had a headache and was trying to medicate himself.

Perhaps Fats could have used a couple of aspirin on those two fall mornings. Who knows? But one thing is certain: Josh's dog did sense trouble each time, and that trouble was an earthquake.

PART IV
Paw Power
Extraordinary Strength
& Endurance

Chapter Twelve

Hold On!

Power to Grasp and Hold Like a Vice

Marley, the mischievous Labrador retriever in John Grogan's bestselling *Marley & Me,* did not chew himself into the hearts of dog owners because his behavior was radically out of the ordinary. Marley tugged at the heartstrings—and tugged with vigor—by behaving precisely as dogs do. That is, with powerful jaws and a ravenous appetite for anything that can be chewed to pieces.

Marley gnawed his way out of crates and through doors. He tried, and made progress, chewing himself out of a garage. If there was an object susceptible to a dog bite, Marley would chomp it. If there was an item seemingly immune from such attacks, he would find a way.

Dog owners relate, because many have similar stories. A frustrated writer asked Miami-area veterinarian Patty Khuly for advice about a border collie that, by age six months, had "chewed through every chair leg in our house" and "even made dents in the aluminum ones outside." The vet began her reply by noting that "a rough estimate for what my own dog has chewed up over the past year of his puppyhood came to just under $3,000."

Boston Red Sox relief pitcher Jonathan Papelbon's dog, Boss, did more financial damage than that in devouring the baseball that Papelbon used to record the final out in Boston's 2007 World Series championship. "He jumped up one day on the counter and snatched it," Papelbon said. "He likes rawhide. He tore that thing to pieces.... I'll keep what's left of it."

Average, ordinary household dogs have chewed through wire fences, solid wood doors, and even thick walls. The Web site *dogbreedinfo.com* solicited photos of dogs "caught in the act." At last check, the site offered more than twenty Web pages filled with submitted photos of dogs caught in various forms of mischief, many involving chewed-up toys, furniture, Christmas trees, and the like.

Dogs have extremely powerful jaws and strong, often sharp teeth—forty-two of them, to be exact. The incisive teeth cut, the molars break and chew, and the force at which dogs use them allows them to get through even some of the hardest materials. After all, the ancestors of domestic dogs needed to catch, hold, and kill prey if they wanted to eat. Training dogs to use their choppers in nondestructive ways is now an almost universal challenge for owners.

Owners like John Bernin can relate. A documentary filmmaker from Evanston, Illinois, Bernin has owned well-behaved dogs that have fetched newspapers for treats and could be left in open-door houses with no worries. And then there was Ashley. Ashley was a Weimaraner with a severe case of separation anxiety. She would sometimes "escape" out the front door only to find her way to the back of the house and dig her way under a fence to get back inside. The dog's chewing meant stays in the Bernin basement whenever the family left the house. Ashley would go downstairs willingly enough; it's just that the sixty-pound pooch had no interest in staying there for long.

The moment the front door closed, the chewing began. Ashley chewed through a three-quarter-inch wooden door to escape the first time. On another occasion, she chewed off a steel doorknob until the lock "popped." When troubled with the knob, she tried to chew her way through the walls surrounding the door.

"She just wouldn't stop," Bernin recalls.

After their first several attempts to contain the dog failed, the Bernins gave up on buying new doorknobs. Instead, they purchased sheet metal and laminated it to the downstairs side of the basement door. Presumably, Ashley would not be able to get past the metal barrier to the wood.

Somehow, she did.

When Bernin returned home, he went to the basement. Ashley had used her jaws and paws to pry a corner of the metal off the door, then kept gnawing at it—and the wood—until she was bleeding. "Fortunately," Bernin said, "she came out of it okay."

Some dog breeds, depending largely on the shape of the jaw, can exert a bite force exceeding three hundred pounds per square inch (psi). On average, humans exert approximately half that force. Alligators remain the kings of mammal jaw power, at more than 2,000 psi—about the strength of a mid-sized sedan falling on something, according to a study by the *Journal of Zoology of London*. While the idea that some dog breeds can "lock" their jaws is a myth, items caught in the grip of a pit bull terrier or Rottweiler bite might feel otherwise.

"Some dogs just seem addicted to chewing," says animal behaviorist Cheryl Falkenburry. "Everything in the house is considered a chew toy in their mind."

The same might be said for the sheet metal, doorknobs, or plywood that Ashley, the Evanston Weimaraner, put in her vise-like jaws. Bernin will never forget the power of his dog.

"She lived to be twelve," he said, thinking back to the sad day in 2007 when he and his family had to put Ashley down. "Then we remodeled the whole house."

Chapter Thirteen

Nothing Like a Fur Coat

Power to Endure the Cold

A dog's average body temperature is a few degrees higher than that of a human. Dogs hover in the 101–102.5 range, compared to your own 98.6. Straight mathematics, then, would suggest that extremely cold weather should affect dogs more harshly than it does humans. Dogs, after all, are accustomed to functioning with warmer blood coursing through their systems.

Don't tell that to fans of sled dog racing, to owners of an Akita or a Newfoundland, or to anyone who has enjoyed a winter day romping through the snow with the family pet. Warm blood aside, dogs enjoy a unique power to handle cold weather, and it's more than their fur coats that keeps them warm.

Dogs' ancestors—wolves—have bristly, stiff hairs surrounding their toes that insulate and provide traction. In addition, wolves sleep on cold nights with their tails wrapped around their noses, trapping their warm breath in a foot-warming heater of sorts. While domesticated dogs have lost some of these survival traits through the generations, most do handle cold weather better than their 98.6-degree human counterparts. This is especially true of certain breeds.

Breeds like the keeshond and Akita have thick coats to insulate them from heat loss in cold climates. The German shepherd has a double-hair coat that serves the same purpose. Other breeds, like the Newfoundland and Saint Bernard, have the additional advantage of massive size to help them thrive in chilly weather.

Another powerful trait that gives dogs a warming advantage over humans involves blood flow. When people are poorly insulated in cold weather, the body slows down blood flow to the feet and hands, instead surrounding the vital organs. That's why warm boots and gloves are important in cold weather (yes, your mother was right), and why frostbite almost always begins in the human extremities.

Dogs' circulatory systems are set up to exchange heat, the warm blood carrying oxygen to their limbs flows in arteries right next to the veins that return the colder blood from the limbs, warming it in the process. This lessens the loss of heat in the exposed parts of canine feet and allows dogs to maintain their body temperature for longer stretches of time in cold climes.

That's not to say that dogs should not be protected in cold weather. In fact, veterinarians stress that keeping dogs—particularly small ones, and ones without "winter coats"—insulated in winter weather is very important.

Northern settlers used to survive cold nights by nuzzling up to their dogs. In addition to offering their higher-than human body temperatures, dogs like to sleep in packs, or while cuddling up to people. Research done by anthropologist Richard Gould in the 1960s found that aborigines in Australia used tamed dingoes in this same manner.

"Some arctic tribes in Russia, such as the Samoyeds (who gave their name to the handsome white Nordic dog) commonly do the same," asserts Stanley Coren in *Why Does My Dog Act That Way?* "Early in the twentieth century, in Newfoundland, the practice was to tuck a dog under the blankets to warm a bed on cold nights, and thus came the tradition of describing a cold period as 'a three-dog night,' meaning that it was so cold that you would need three dogs to keep warm."

Perhaps the greatest story of dogs' power to survive frigid conditions is a famous one, and led to the most well-known of sled dog races.

In January 1925, a diphtheria outbreak in Nome, Alaska, threatened to kill several of the town's young people. The only serum that could help was nearly one thousand miles away in Anchorage, and the only aircraft capable of delivering the medicine quickly had been shut down for the winter.

Sled dogs were the last resort—the only option, though many wondered whether the journey was possible. More than twenty mushers took part in a relay through the worst kinds of conditions. Winds were strong enough to blow some of the dogs right off their feet. Temperatures were subfreezing most of the way.

Remarkably, just six days after the first team left Anchorage, lead dog Balto and musher Gunner Kaassen sledded into Nome on February 2, 1925, saving lives and earning the husky and his team a hero's welcome. After Balto's death eight years later, his body was preserved and displayed at Cleveland's Natural History Museum. A statue of Balto was erected in New York's Central Park.

Today, teams of dogs make the run on the Iditarod Trail for sport. The Iditarod, run annually, is sled dog racing's signature event, and it's no wonder the dogs seem to hold up better in the frigid conditions than some of the mushers and spectators do—even with their heavy workload.

It's not just in their fur coats. It's in their blood. And it's a powerful ability indeed.

Chapter Fourteen

They've Got Pull

Power to Pull and Haul Heavy Loads

Some dogs are strong and some dogs are fast, but a dog's amazing ability to haul heavy loads over long distances is the result of incredible strength and endurance. When it comes to load-hauling, nothing matches the super-dog powers of far-northern dog breeds.

Northern breeds are great at hauling loads because, for millennia, they needed to haul their human masters all over the arctic. Nowadays, popular weight-pulling and sledding competitions showcase this canine superpower. The most famous of these is the Alaskan Iditarod Trail Sled Dog Race, in which dogs pull their masters (known as "mushers") over 1,161 miles of rugged Alaskan territory. In the 2011 race, musher John Baker and his dogs traveled the entire course in less than eight days, 19 hours, an achievement that remains the Iditarod record.

But amazing load-hauling feats are not limited to the Iditarod. On October 21, 2000, a team of 210 sledding huskies pulled off an equally impressive world record: They towed a Kenworth truck and flatbed trailer with a load weighing 145,002 pounds a full six blocks up a street in Whitehorse, Yukon Territory. Still not impressed? In one weight-pulling competition, a single Alaskan malamute pulled a 3,300-pound load—about the weight of an automobile. In order for a malamute to even be eligible for the coveted Alaskan Malamute Club of America Working Weight Pulling Dog title, it has to be able to pull a *minimum* of eight times its weight.

Such amazing tales of the endurance of dogs are common in polar regions. Native Inuit populations, from Alaska to Siberia, relied on dogs to support their nomadic lifestyle. Naturalist J. Dewey Soper once wrote that "it is difficult to visualize that there ever was a time in their struggle for existence during which the Eskimo found it possible to cope with the conditions of a polar environment without their dogs." The Inuit traversed harsh lands in search of diffuse food sources, meaning they continuously moved about all the provisions of their village. Inuit dog breeds became load-hauling machines.

The exploits of Inuit dogs make the tenacity of a pit bull or the strength of a German shepherd seem like kid's stuff. In 1975 legendary Inuit hunter Tatigat returned to his village after a month of hunting with his family. Heaped onto one sled were fourteen caribou carcasses, two seals, thirty dried seal skins, two wooden boxes of tools, two trunks, caribou hide blankets, and

Tatigat's wife and two children. This hefty load was carried more than 130 kilometers by fourteen sledge dogs in seventeen hours. Moreover, conditions were abysmal. It was -22 degrees Fahrenheit. Northern hauling dogs are mostly husky breeds, and the secret to their endurance begins with their evolution from the gray wolf. Most scientists believe that dogs evolved from wolves around 13,000 years ago, when the end of the last ice age was about to set in. Food sources became scarce for both humans and wolves. Theory has it that some hungry wolves scavenged for scraps around human encampments. The bravest approached the humans, begging for food. Over time, these wolf scavengers evolved into dogs. From there, humans selectively bred dogs, hence the variant breeds that exist today.

The characteristics that humans—and nature—select for depend on the given environment. In polar climes, domesticated dogs needed to withstand cold and travel long distances, all while towing the belongings of their human masters. Breeds like the Siberian husky, the Samoyed, the Canadian Eskimo dog, and the Alaskan malamute all have thick insulating fur and snouts that warm the air as they breathe. These breeds are more closely related to wolves than are most dogs, yet with additional adaptations that make them better load-haulers than even the strongest of wolves.

The real secret to load-hauling stamina is efficient energy use. All dogs are great at storing heat and energy, but not so great at getting rid of it. The more mass a dog has, the more energy it produces. The ability to get rid of this heat, meanwhile, is not proportional to mass, but proportional to the surface area of the dog's body. Since large dogs have a larger mass-to-surface area ratio than smaller dogs, large dogs have proportionally less surface area to radiate their heat. Inuit dog breeds evolved to be muscular yet lean, so they can efficiently expend energy while running and hauling and also survive days at a time without eating—vital in the polar regions, where food supply is unpredictable.

As sledding dogs are used more often for racing rather than hauling—where speed trumps strength—racing dogs become less muscular and more lean. When the Iditarod race began in 1973, most of the dogs were still real load-hauling dogs. They were heavier than the Iditarod dogs of today, which are bred and trained to get from Point A to Point B as quickly as possible. Modern Iditarod dogs have such amazing strength and stamina for their size that Iditarod champion Martin Buser deems the ideal racing dog "a fifty-pound dog with a hundred-pound heart."

While hauling their loads, sledding dogs can burn up to ten thousand calories a day. Scientists suspect there is still much to be discovered about the amazing endurance of these dogs. Erica McKenzie, a research professor of veterinary medicine at Oregon State University, thinks sledding dogs tap into an energy source called blood globulins once they run out of other sources of energy. In reference to dogs in Alaskan sled races, McKenzie explains, "when human marathon runners run out of glycogen, they hit the wall. When racing dogs run out, they seem to find another source, and we think blood globulins may provide part of that source."

The loads of polar dog breeds have been dwindling lately. There was once a time when dog-sled teams delivered the mail to villages across the arctic, and indigenous communities and their dogs crisscrossed their territories by foot and sled alone. While there are still pockets of native communities that use dogs for traditional duties, airplanes and snowmobiles have mostly taken up the load-hauling burden. But in the event of emergency, sled dogs can still be counted on to get whatever is needed from Point A to Point B.

PART V
Doctor Dog
Power of Healing

Chapter Fifteen

On Red Alert

Power to Detect Oncoming Seizures

When she was seventeen years old, Candice Hernandez feared for her life. For unknown reasons, she began suffering seizures—and they wouldn't stop.

Candice was enduring dozens of seizures a week, each one lasting about fifteen to twenty minutes. She spent many days in the hospital and missed most of her senior year in high school.

Doctors responded with vagus nerve stimulation (VNS) therapy. They implanted a device into Candice's chest, which when activated (with a special magnet) sent electrical impulses to the vagus nerve in the neck. By activating the device before a seizure started, Candice could greatly control the seizure's effects. Only one problem:

She wasn't always able to predict when the seizure would begin. If it gripped her body while she was climbing stairs or involved in some other activity, she could seriously hurt herself. Luckily, Chiper came into Candice's life. Part German shepherd, Chiper had a remarkable talent: She could predict when her owner was about to have a seizure. After proper training, Chiper would lick Candice's hand about twenty minutes before the onset of her seizure. And that's not all.

"After I have a seizure, I get really disoriented," Candice says. "And if I try to stand up and walk around, I'm likely to fall and hurt myself. Chiper lies on me and pins me down, and she won't let me stand up until I'm back to normal."

Chiper was both a seizure-response dog and a seizure-alert dog. The former type of dog is heroic, while the latter is seemingly miraculous.

In the United States, more than 2.3 million people suffer from epileptic seizures. Many dogs become frightened when their owner has a seizure, and they themselves have to be calmed down. But seizure-response dogs are trained to help. Organizations such as Canine Partners for Life teach dogs how to respond during their owners' seizures. Some are trained to press a large button on a phone that dials 9-1-1. Seizure-response dogs press up to their owners to keep them from hurting themselves in case they fall. These dogs carry medical supplies when they leave the home, and they rouse their owners if they become unconscious. Just by being "on call," the dogs help their owners feel more assured and confident.

Then there are the seizure-*alert* dogs, which

seem to have fallen from Heaven. These dogs can predict their owner's seizure twenty minutes, forty minutes, or even more than an hour before the attack. Many Americans first became aware of such dogs in the mid-1980s, when news reports circulated about an epileptic woman in the state of Washington. The woman insisted that a dog she worked with always knew when she was going to have a seizure.

In the early 1990s, renowned dog expert Roger A. Caras told the story of Sheba, a dog that sensed when thirteen-year-old Angie was going to have a seizure. Caras, who was also a reporter for ABC News, brought a camera crew to tape Sheba in action. With the cameras rolling, Sheba barked, grabbed Angie's hand, and pulled her toward the couch, where she would be safe. Trusting in Sheba's prediction, Angie lay on the couch in the fetal position in preparation for the seizure. Sheba then jumped on Angie's body and laid her head next to the girl's nose and mouth. Caras reveals: "Angie's mother knew that if her daughter's breathing in any way faltered, Sheba would detect it even quicker than she could and give the alarm."

After reading about Angie's story, author Tiffin Shew-make researched old magazines and newspapers and found other stories about dogs predicting seizures—including one article from 1875. But only since the 1990s have trainers, such as Sharon Hermansen of the Canine Seizure Assist Society of North Carolina, formally trained seizure-alert dogs.

Not every dog is blessed with this "magical power." In fact, only a small percentage—about

10 percent, according to some reports—seem capable of seizure detection. The behavior has been seen in collies, border collies, German shepherds, Labradors, and Shih Tzus.

Dr. Roger Reep, an anatomist and physiologist at the University of Florida's College of Veterinary Medicine, believes that alert dogs can smell changes in their handler's body prior to a seizure. According to Reep, the electrical activity in the brain that initiates the seizure begins up to ninety minutes before the patient begins to tremble. The activity occurs in the area of the brain that controls such involuntary responses as heartbeat and perspiration.

Says Reep: "We think alerting dogs can not only detect the odor but they can hook it up with some idea [that] the person is in danger. And we think that's tied to having a close bond between the dog and the owner so the dog is motivated to protect the person's well-being."

Alert dogs also possess a similar trait: They are typically hyperactive and vigilant—in need of something to do throughout the day and night. An alert dog would rather sniff and react to body changes than lay around like a couch potato.

Today, there are hundreds of trained seizure-alert dogs in the world, including a Shih Tzu named Precious in Santa Cruz, California. Precious predicts Cyndi Davenport's seizures forty-five minutes before they occur, running to Cyndi's mother, Jan, in such situations. "It's a miracle," Jan says. "I can't say anything else."

Then there is teenager Kristina Potts of Columbus, Indiana, who feels more confident now that Sparky is at her side.

"He knows before I have a seizure and 'tells' my mom," Kristina says. During Kristina's seizures, Sparky lies next to her and licks her face until she wakes up. Because Kristina tends to drop things throughout the day because of tremors, Sparky was trained to pick things up for her. "I can be more independent with Sparky there to take care of me," Kristina says. "He is my best friend."

Chapter Sixteen

The Autistic's Little Helper

Power to Mitigate Autism Symptoms

"Bye, brown shoes."

The words were uttered by a young boy with autism not to a man with brown shoes, but to a dog. Spree was a brown-footed German shepherd owned by Kaylan Head, whose Full Circle Obedience School in Oklahoma City has trained therapy dogs and champion obedience and agility dogs since 1990.

Unlike some of Head's more subtle four-footed friends who were known for their work with autistic children, Spree would lick, nudge, bark, or paw at the children until they paid some attention. This particular boy, while refusing to speak, stretched out his legs near

Spree's, eyed the dog's feet, and then touched his own small brown shoe.

"She has brown shoes like you," Head told the autistic boy, whose teacher was watching in amazement at the focus the child was showing toward the dog. Head continued talking to the young boy, but he did not seem to be listening to her.

When it was time to leave, Head and Spree said goodbye and turned toward the exit. From behind them, they were surprised to hear the boy's voice for the first time.

"Bye, brown shoes."

"It was such a soft voice," Head recalled in 2008. "Such a small thing—three syllables. But it has stuck with me for fifteen years."

Autism is a developmental disability marked by impairment in social interaction and communication as well as the presence of unusual interests and behaviors, according to the United States Department of Health and Human Services. Many people with autism also have unusual ways of learning, paying attention, and reacting to various sensations.

Autistic disorders are mysterious, to be sure. While most doctors believe both genes and the environment can play a role, much is unknown about the causes of autism. In the same way, treatments vary widely in both their method and their success in helping autistic patients "connect" with others socially.

If only dogs could talk, we might gain clues about what actually does work.

"It's well known that [autistic individuals] are generally repelled by humans who try to connect with them," maintains Lynn Hoover, author and certified dog behavior consultant in Pittsburgh who has seen the profound effect dogs can have on those with autism. "There's far more that repels than amuses a person with autism.

"However, many individuals with autism have this attraction to dogs, so strong that they want to 'bridge' with dogs. It helps if the dog is trained to serve, but just being a dog provides magic enough for some children and adults challenged by autism. It's through dogs that some autistic [people] are drawn to connect."

"I'm sure there's some sort of scientific explanation for it," offers Karen Shirk, whose Ohio-based 4 Paws for Ability nonprofit service pairs service dogs with the disabled and specializes in helping children with autism. "But I call it magic."

Actually, scientific explanation is evasive at best.

Some service dog trainers who work with the autistic emphasize that dogs tend to obey better with eye contact. They encourage those with autism to make such a connection with their four-legged helpers. For many with autism, eye contact that is elusive around teachers, family, and others comes more easily with dogs. For some, that connection with a dog provides reassurance and confidence.

In 2013, Francesca Cirulli of the National Institute of Health in Rome, Italy, discussed recent studies regarding dogs' effects on children with autism. Cirulli found that in one study, kids were more talkative and socially engaged when a therapy dog was present. In another study, just of boys, the kids smiled more and were less aggressive when a therapy dog was in the room.

Head speculates that autistic children and dogs have a great deal in common, particularly when it comes to body language. For example, she points out that many dogs prefer to avoid eye contact, go rigid in stressful situations, and use repetitive motion to calm themselves. Perhaps there is some logic, then, in why autistic children and dogs "take" to one another. It's not just a one-way dynamic. Head's dogs "had a much different attitude, happier, when working with autistic children than with physically ill children, or with the elderly," she recalls.

Shirk also points to the unconditional emotional support that a dog provides as a particular help to those with autism. Many with autism tend to isolate themselves from others. "For our children with autism," she says, "their dog might be the only friend that they have."

Hoover taught an effervescent poodle to lie on top of a five-year-old autistic boy to provide "tactile stimulation"—structured touch designed to foster development. It calmed the boy, who had been thrashing around in the dentist's chair, making a routine check of his teeth seemingly impossible. With the poodle on his chest, he calmed down and allowed the dentist to do the job.

The same poodle once coaxed a loud laugh when, as the boy was taking a bath, the dog took advantage of the opportunity to snatch his clothes from the floor and dash off with them. "What sport," Hoover describes. "And like magic, puppy hijinks made the boy laugh. Just by being himself, this dog worked his magic on the child."

Head heard similar laughter when her whippet, Trax, would visit an Oklahoma hospital. With many patients, Trax would make full eye contact. With the autistic, the dog seemed to know that turning his head and body sideways and "scooting" into them was the more effective approach. Many of the children would then reach out and explore his ears and nose. She would dress the dog, particularly at holiday time, and marvel at the way the children reacted.

One eleven-year-old boy would drop to the floor as soon as he saw the dogs arrive, and would laugh when Trax plopped down right beside him. It was, Head recalls, "the kind of laugh that started as a barely audible giggle, and would rise to a loud and continuous cackle. It was infectious. The most stern and serious workers would pause and watch for a few seconds, then walk away smiling.

"The caregivers said that was the only time the boy was ever observed laughing."

The joy of a child laughing. Or uttering three simple words: "Bye, brown shoes."

Powerful reactions, thanks to the power of dogs.

Chapter Seventeen

The Friendly Picker-Upper

Power to Overcome Depression

Years ago, veterinarian Jack Stephens owned a pet store with his wife, Vicki. One day, a sad, lonely widower came by looking to buy a puppy. The man had never shown much interest in dogs, but he bought one anyway. Perhaps, he thought, it might help him cope with his dreary life. He had no friends or relatives nearby, and he faced an upcoming surgery for prostate cancer.

After the operation, the man's primary physician worried that he would recover slowly due to his long history of depression. But the man recovered quickly and, according to Vicki, he seemed happier and more confident than when he had first entered the store. He also had made friends during his now-frequent walks around the neighborhood. The doctor asked the man what had transformed him.

"Buster," he replied.

"What is a Buster?" the doctor asked.

"Buster," the man said, "is my new puppy!"

All over the world, dogs are lifting the spirits of the sad and the lonely, the grieving and the clinically depressed. Many dogs will try to comfort their owners when they're crying, offering not a tissue but a paw. Some dogs will literally lick people's tears away, turning frowns into chuckles and smiles.

During America's darkest hour, the tragedy of 9/11, dogs across the country helped people cope with the heavy sorrow. "Many of my family and friends were affected by the events that took place in New York City," offers Audrey Pavia, the former managing editor of *Dog Fancy* magazine, "and a childhood friend of my husband's was killed in the World Trade Center. My depression those first two weeks after the attacks knew no bounds."

Fortunately, Pavia had a corgi to help her get through each day. "Nigel was still a puppy," she recalls, "and completely oblivious to what was happening around him. He was still happy and wiggly, full of kisses and comic antics. He still needed to be cared for, and still asked for his daily walks. With Nigel to care for and constantly reminding me that life goes on, I was eventually able to lift myself from my terrible sadness."

In recent years, the medical community has embraced the use of pets—particularly dogs—in the treatment of depression. In 2007, the National Women's Health Resource Center ran a national education campaign dedicated to people with depression. The organization touted the benefits of a dog to help cope with the illness.

Stephens, a happy owner of eight dogs and two cats, actively supports the idea. Stephens notes a study performed by the University of Missouri School of Veterinary Medicine and Nursing. Researchers found that those who petted a dog for twenty minutes experienced an increase in serotonin—a brain chemical that regulates mood. Those with low serotonin suffer from depression, so the lesson was clear: Get a pup, and your serotonin goes up.

Those who are seriously depressed might not be capable of training, walking, or fulfilling their canine's basic needs. But if they are capable, then a dog might be just what the doctor ordered. A dog can not only improve his owner's serotonin level but also promote the release of endorphins. Specifically, *exercise* helps us produce brain chemicals called *endorphins,* which lead to *euphoria*—or at least a general state of wellbeing. Most dogs prompt us to exercise. In fact, many dogs insist that we roll out of bed, get off the couch, and snap their leash on. They need to go to the bathroom and, while they're at it, walk around the block.

Exercise not only makes us more "euphoric" but it helps us feel more relaxed and feel better about ourselves. It may also put us in better contact with our neighbors. Jack London, a cartoonist, suffered from depression until he adopted a stray dog. "Thor introduced me to people," London reveals. "People will open up to a cute dog faster than they will a human, hence they open up to the human as well."

Dogs also provide friendship. Unlike turtles and goldfish, dogs thrive on interaction with humans. You can play fetch with dogs, watch TV with them, and check out that strange noise in the basement together. Though you can't have a conversation with Scruffy, you can always talk to her and she'll always listen. Stephens especially recommends dogs for depressed individuals who live by themselves, since dogs greatly help people cope with loneliness.

And that's not all. Contends Dr. Kristie Leong, M.D., "Having a dog or cat that needs care and nurturing helps to raise the self-esteem of a depressed person." Those who feel "worth-less" and "lost" might find that taking care of a dog adds value and structure to their lives. By providing two meals and three walks a day, they are helping a fellow creature live and thrive. Such responsibility can give a person a sense of purpose.

Dogs allow us to express our love to them, which can be good training for our human relationships. And, of course, the love they give back can do a world of good. "Dogs provide unconditional love—something depressed people often need," Pavia writes. "Because dogs are non-judgmental, people who are depressed know they can always turn to their dogs for love and companionship when the rest of the world seems too complicated to help them."

Dogs make us feel wanted and special, especially when we walk in the door. They reach up to us with their paws and lick our faces if we let them. They also are an endless source of amusement, whether they're trying to dig a Cheerio out of the couch cushions or looking at you out of the corner of their eyes when they're pretending to pout. They "wag and yodel in happiness," writes dog breeder Chris Walkowicz, and "comfort us with kisses or nudges when we're sad."

In recent years, therapy dogs have been used to treat people with depression. Some of these dogs visit hospitals, nursing homes, and other facilities, where they bring cheer and comfort to the infirm and the elderly. Some therapy dogs live with those suffering from depression. Some have been trained to lick the tears of their owners if they are crying and even bring them tissues. If their masters appear apathetic, therapy dogs have been taught to initiate play.

Certainly, those suffering from depression need medical attention, but they also could benefit from a visit to the breeder. Dogs like Buster have been known to change lives.

—Chapter Eighteen—
Stress-Busters

Power to Lower Our Blood Pressure

Terry Seraceno, head of Dr. Paws Therapy Dogs, was leaving a hospital with her two therapeutic dogs when she heard screaming and crying. The dogs heard the cries too, and they pulled Terry and her partner, Denise, toward the ailing patient, a thirteen-year-old girl. The young teen, lying on a gurney outside the Emergency Room entrance, was suffering from a terribly painful headache after undergoing a spinal tap. Terry and Denise, and apparently the dogs, felt bad for the ailing girl.

"She glanced over to us as we asked her if she'd like a visit from the Dr. Paws Therapy Dogs," Seraceno recalls. "She slowed down her sobbing and saw a golden retriever and a Chihuahua. The nurse and mother asked if we could stay." Seraceno had to get back home, but Denise

95

stayed with the girl. With the dogs at her side, the girl became more and more relaxed.

"Denise later told me that they were able to control her crying and pain long enough to get a better assessment and blood pressure on the child," Saraceno says. "By the time the doctor got around to seeing her, the Chihuahua was on her lap and she was sitting up in the bed; the crying had almost stopped. Even though she was still in pain, she didn't seem to notice as much."

The dogs were working such wonders that the doctor asked Denise to keep them there as the girl was being treated. As the Dr. Paws women know, dogs help lower people's levels of anxiety, stress, and blood pressure—and more.

Members of the American Heart Association learned about these extra powers in November 2005. At an AHA meeting in Dallas, a new study was discussed concerning dogs and heart patients. Kathie Cole, a nurse at the UCLA Medical Center, showed that therapeutic dogs helped patients who were suffering from heart failure. Simply by being kind pals, the dogs improved the patients' heart and lung function. And as with the thirteen-year-old girl, they decreased the patients' levels of anxiety and stress, which lowered their blood pressure.

How do these special animals work such magic? "How, I don't know," says dog trainer and author Chris Walkowicz. "But it works. All I have to do in my doctor's office is *think* about petting my dog while the nurse is taking my b.p.!"

No doctor can fully explain, in scientific terms, how the dogs perform such miracles. But the data from Cole's study, and others, don't lie.

Petting a friendly dog makes a person feel happier, calmer, more relaxed. "You can see it on their face," says Cole. "First you see a smile and then you see the worries of the world roll off their shoulders."

In Cole's study, seventy-six heart failure patients were visited by either a volunteer, a volunteer with a dog, or no one at all. Patients' levels of epinephrine, a hormone that the body makes when the person is stressed, dropped by 2 percent when only the volunteer came to visit. But when a dog came along, the epinephrine fell a whopping 17 percent—more than eightfold! Moreover, the patients' heart pressure and lung pressure dropped when the dog showed up; 10 percent and 5 percent, respectively. When just the volunteer arrived, heart and lung pressure actually rose. In addition, the patients' anxiety level—determined by a standard rating scale—plummeted an average of 24 percent after visiting with the pooches.

Dr. Marc Gillinov, a cardiac surgeon at the world-renowned Cleveland Clinic, embraces the study's findings. "I'm not surprised at all that something that makes people feel good also makes them feel less anxious, has measurable physiological effects," he says.

Doctors have been studying pets' effects on people's health for several decades. In 1979, the University of Pennsylvania School of Veterinary Medicine launched the Center for the Interaction of Animals and Society. Two years later, their findings made headlines in *The Philadelphia Inquirer*. The center claimed that "companion animals" (i.e., pets) could help lower their owners' blood pressure.

Dr. Alan M. Beck, director of the center, said in 1981: "We've shown in the laboratory that petting an animal calms the nervous system and lowers blood pressure in hypertensive subjects. And recent studies have demonstrated that the survival rate of heart attack victims is significantly higher among pet owners than non-owners."

In 1999, scientists showed that dogs can even tackle heavy-duty stress. Researchers at State University of New York at Buffalo studied forty-eight stockbrokers, all of whom were taking a medication for hypertension (high blood pressure). In the experiment, half of the brokers were given a pet. All of the brokers were then put through simulated stressful situations. For example, they had to calm an irate client who had just lost $86,000 in the stock market.

The researchers discovered that the brokers with pets were better at keeping their cool. For them, the stress-related increase in blood pressure was much lower than for those in the other group. "Those who had pets went from 120 to 126 for systolic blood pressure," says psychologist Karen Allen, who helped lead the study. "Those who had no pets went from 120 to about 148."

Other studies have produced similar results. In one study, researchers examined ninety-two sufferers of heart attacks or angina, all of whom were hospitalized in coronary care units. One year later, the researchers checked on their status. Twenty-eight percent of those who were not pet owners were dead. Among those who lived with a dog or other pet, only six percent had passed away.

Results from such studies have convinced some hospital executives to welcome four-legged visitors. UCLA runs a program called People Animal Connection, in which therapeutic dogs visit hospital patients and inevitably raise their spirits. Participants include soulful Labradors, floppy sheepdogs, and playful mutts who hop on children's beds. Jack Barron, the program's director, firmly believes in the healing power of dogs.

"These wonderful, wonderful animals give us so much," Barron raves in the program's promotional video. "They don't ask anything. It's just unconditional love. They don't care if you're a man or a woman, a child, an old person—it doesn't matter. It doesn't matter where you come from. We put these guys on the patients' beds and they make sad faces turn to happy faces."

In 2008, a study in Israel revealed that dogs helped lower the blood pressure of children. Researchers from several institutions examined nearly 230 first-, second-, and third-graders. They found that the eighty-five children who lived with dogs had blood pressures that were, on average, 4.5 mercury-millimeters lower than those who didn't have dogs—a significant difference considering the large size of the sample groups.

Dr. Michael Bailash, who headed the study, suggested that children with dogs get more exercise than other kids—be it roughhousing with their pet in the living room or going for walks with their pups. He added that dogs, at times, might be the child's only calming influence in the family. "[Dogs] won't steal your toys like a brother or sister," Bailash says, "or yell at you for not doing your homework like your mother or father."

Of course, dogs are not *always* stress reducers. Anyone who has tried to train a Jack Russell puppy knows that. In addition, poorly trained dogs might whine, howl, bark, or paw at the table during mealtime, making the already tension-filled family dinner even more stressful. Then there are those people who fear dogs. For them, a canine's presence gets their heart pumping.

Yet for most people, dogs provide a wonderful calming effect. Alfredo Castaneda, a twenty-seven-year-old heart transplant candidate in 2005, felt at peace when a golden retriever lay next to him on his hospital bed. "Having him here makes me forget everything else for a little bit," Castaneda said. "It's beautiful."

Raymond Galmiche knows the feeling. A Vietnam War veteran living in Williston, Florida, Galmiche suffered from post-traumatic stress disorder and high anxiety. In 2011, he was introduced to a German shepherd named Dazzle through Guardian Angels Medical Service Dogs, Inc. "What he does for me is focuses on problems I experience," Galmiche told *The Gainesville Sun* in 2013. "He calms me and keeps me grounded. He's an amazing, amazing animal, and I love him."

—Chapter Nineteen—
Cancer Detectors

Power to Diagnose the Disease

Nancy, a mother of three, ran a successful coffeehouse in California. Despite her busy days, she always set aside time to play with her dog, Mia. One day in 2000, however, Mia began a bizarre sequence of behavior, as she started sniffing at Nancy's breast. The next night, the dog pulled the bed covers off Nancy and snapped at her shirt. The following day, she repeated this obsessive behavior. When Mia jumped on her owner's chest, Nancy felt a pain in her breast. Her physician confirmed what the dog had already sensed: Nancy had breast cancer.

For years we had heard that dogs had the power to detect cancer, but no one had actually proven the theory until recently. In 2006, Michael McCulloch, research director for the Pine

Street Foundation in San Anselmo, California, made international headlines with a startling discovery: Ordinary dogs could detect early-stage breast and lung cancers simply by sniffing the breath of those afflicted.

McCulloch worked from the premise that cancer cells release molecules that are different from those of their healthy counterparts. He theorized that dogs, with their highly sensitive noses, could smell the difference between the normal cells and the cancer cells. In McCulloch's study, three Labrador retrievers and two Portuguese water dogs were trained to respond differently to breath samples (sealed in tubes) of healthy people and cancer patients. "The dogs learned to sit or lie down in front of cancer patient samples and to ignore control samples through the method of food reward," McCulloch says.

After training, the dogs were given breath samples from fifty-five people with lung cancer, thirty-one with breast cancer, and eighty-three who were cancer free. It turned out that the dogs correctly distinguished the breath samples of cancer patients from those of the healthy patients in well more than 90 percent of the cases. The dogs also proved capable of detecting the difference between lung and breast cancers. Nicholas Broffman, executive director of the Pine Street Foundation, holds hope that dogs can "detect cancer at its earliest stages, before it even shows up on magnetic resonance imaging [MRI]."

Moreover, it appears that dogs can detect other forms of cancer besides those in the breast or lung. The medical journal *The Lancet* reported that a woman's dog had alerted her to the presence of melanoma (skin cancer) by constantly sniffing the lesion on her leg. Other studies have shown that dogs can detect bladder cancer.

According to a study discussed in the *British Medical Journal* in 2006, ordinary dogs were presented with samples of urine from bladder cancer patients and from people who didn't have bladder cancer. By an overwhelming margin, the dogs were able to detect the difference between the two sets of urine.

"It might be that the dogs are better than our current machines at picking up abnormal proteins in the urine," says David Neal, a bladder and prostate cancer surgeon at Cambridge University in England. "What are the dogs picking up? Can we get a machine that does the same?"

Yes, believes organic chemist George Preti. As reported in 2013, researchers at the University of Pennsylvania's Working Dog Center were training three dogs to detect the signature compound that indicates the presence of ovarian cancer. If the canines could isolate the chemical marker, scientists at Monell Chemical Senses Center would work to create an electronic sensor to identify the same smell. "Because if the dogs can do it," Preti told NBC News, "then the question is, Can our analytical instrumentation do it? We think we can."

James Walker, director of Florida State University's Sensory Research Institute, is not surprised by dogs' cancer-sniffing ability, saying that a dog's nose can detect odors 10,000 to 100,000 times better than a human's nose can.

Research indicates that dogs have a greater variety of smelling receptors in their noses than people do. They also have a greater convergence of neurons from the nose to the brain. "It is clear that the dog has a much greater proportion of its brain devoted to smell than is the case with humans," Walker says.

McCulloch's findings in 2006 were expected to inspire similar and more refined studies. Some believe that physicians may one day employ cancer-sniffing dogs to examine patients—before an invasive and highly risky biopsy, or an expensive MRI, is ordered. McCulloch believes his findings could be revolutionary. "I hope people will be interested in pursuing this research," he says. "It shows that there is definitely something out there."

In South Korea, scientists are serious about using dogs to detect cancer. In 2008, Seoul National University collaborated with Korean biotechnology firm RNL BIO Co. to clone a cancer-sniffing dog. A female black Lab named Marine was unable to bear puppies. However, Marine's cancer-sniffing skills were so valued that researchers cloned her DNA, resulting in four puppies: Marine-L, Marine-N, Marine-R, and Marine-S.

One topic rarely discussed—but critically important—is a dog's ability to detect a *recurrence* of cancer. In a recent issue of *The Oregonian,* Deborah Wood recalls her visit to her friend Gail's house after Gail had surgery for breast cancer. Deborah brought along her dog, Pogo, whom she assumed would play with Gail's two dogs like she always did. Instead, Pogo uncharacteristically sat on Gail's lap and wouldn't get off.

Deborah realized that this was a bad sign. Days later, Gail's lab results revealed that the surgery had not been completely successful. Cancer remained, and she would have to undergo a second operation.

After that surgery, Deborah and Pogo visited Gail again. This time, Pogo greeted Gail, wagged his tail, and went to play with Gail's two dogs.

"Pogo says you're cured," Deborah told Gail.

The next day, Deborah received the results from the lab work. Gail was cancer free.

Like Deborah, Nancy is a true believer. Her physician said that had Mia not detected her cancer, it could have entered her lymph nodes within a few months—making it far more difficult to treat and possibly fatal. Instead, Nancy can now be hopeful to be around a long, long time, setting aside time each day for Mia, who is not only her reason *for* living, but possibly the reason she *is* living.

—Chapter Twenty—
Lifesavers for Diabetics

Power to Detect Low Blood Sugar

April Farzati couldn't sleep at night. Her three-year-old daughter, Abby, suffered from juvenile diabetes, and the effects were horrific. If Abby's blood sugar level dropped too low, she would suffer violent seizures. "When she has seizures," Farzati told Florida's *Charlotte Sun* in December 2007, "she goes blind, she gets paralyzed. She'll hit and kick. She bites my finger as I try to put icing in her mouth." After the seizures, Farzati said, "she looks like she had a stroke."

Abby's symptoms were particularly severe for a diabetic, and her mother sought the expertise of at least a dozen specialists. However, the most critical role in Abby's care was monitoring her blood sugar level. If it got too low, she needed to eat. If it rose too high, she needed insulin. But Farzati, a single mother, needed to work and, of course, sleep. Who would possibly be able to watch Abby up to twenty-four hours a day and, at the same time, determine when her blood sugar was too low or too high?

There was only one kind of creature who could, and it came with four paws.

Farzati heard about Heaven Scent Paws, a Missouri-based company that trained dogs to live with diabetics and react when their blood sugar was out of balance. Incredibly, "diabetic alert service dogs" can scent changes within diabetics' bodies. In fact, they can scent the change in blood sugar a full fifteen minutes before a blood test reveals that change. Moreover, the dogs learn how to react to those changes. They either alert the diabetic or walk to the diabetic's caregiver and make that person aware.

"The dog is trained to detect when her sugar is low, and it is trained to come and get me out of bed," Farzati said. "I have talked to people who have gone through the program, and they have told me their child has not had a seizure since."

Despite the high cost of these wonder dogs—up to $40,000—they are in huge demand. More than 20 million Americans suffer from diabetes, and so far only a few companies train diabetic alert service dogs. These dogs can be lifesavers for the most serious sufferers, particularly those who are vulnerable, such as children.

For those who suffer from Type 1 diabetes, the pancreas does not produce a hormone called insulin. Insulin is essential because it helps prevent the excessive buildup of glucose (sugar) in the blood. Too much glucose (and too little glucose) can cause health problems and lead to long-term damage of the body. Type 1 diabetics need insulin shots daily to lower their blood sugar, and they need to eat appropriate foods at certain times of the day so that their blood sugar does not drop too low.

If a diabetic's blood sugar falls too low, he or she could suffer a seizure. That is what happened to Michelle Reinkemeyer's young son in 2001. Months after being diagnosed with Type 1 diabetes at age seven, Joseph unleashed a "terrifying and guttural scream" in the middle of the night. "I ran downstairs, loading the shotgun as I went, thinking someone had broken into our home," Reinkemeyer recalls. "There our son lay on the floor unable to talk, eyes rolled back in his head, and thrashing about."

Reinkemeyer and her husband administered a glucagon shot and called 9-1-1. Every night after that, the couple and their seven children went to bed in fear, dreading another seizure. Michelle and her husband got up every hour during the night to check their son's blood sugar and feed him if it was low. Despite their efforts, their son suffered ten more seizures. Once a friendly, outgoing child, he became a cranky recluse who didn't want to be seen in public, for fear people would witness one of his seizures.

Their son's eleventh seizure was particularly horrific. At that point, Michelle Reinkemeyer became a woman on a mission, determined to find help for her son. One day, she came across a story on the Internet about a Saint Bernard service dog who alerted its diabetic owner when her blood sugar was too low. Michelle questioned service dog trainers about this, but they retorted that such training was impossible. Persevering, she read numerous dog-training books and eventually purchased a German shepherd puppy named Delta.

For hours each day, the Reinkemeyers put Delta through scent training exercises related to Joseph's blood sugar. At night, the pup slept in Joseph's bed. In just a matter of days, the dog began alerting Joseph and his parents (who had a baby monitor in his room) when his blood sugar was low. Delta fussed, whined, and licked Joseph's face, signaling to the family that it was time for Joseph to snack. From then on, Joseph no longer had to worry about seizures. He became a happier child and, with Delta always at his side, more confident in public.

It was as if Delta had been sent from Heaven. In fact, after training more diabetic alert service dogs (including one for their diabetic daughter), the Reinkemeyers started a company called Heaven Scent Paws. Employing veterinarians, master trainers, an endocrinologist, and others, the company provided diabetic alert dogs to dozens of families in need. While many of the dogs turned out to be wondrously successful detectors, other dogs didn't, sadly resulting in a class-action lawsuit against the company.

Nevertheless, the Reinkemeyers' discovery has provided hope that someday thousands of dogs could be trained as diabetic companions. A small number of other organizations, and individual dog trainers, are trying to follow the Reinkemeyers' lead. In 2008, diabetic trainer Sara Scott was determined to write a free training guide about how to teach dogs to scent dangerously low blood sugar levels. "I am severely hypoglycemic and have also been suffering from grand mal seizures," Scott writes. "I have trained Ranger, my 10-month-old puppy, to do service tasks (dial a rescue phone, bring me my medications, bring me my cell phone, shut cabinet doors and drawers, etc.)."

In 2008, scientists at Queen's University in Northern Ireland tried to move beyond anecdotal evidence and *prove* that dogs could detect a drop in blood sugar. In the meantime, more and more success stories are emerging.

Teenager Grace Hanks was considered a "brittle" diabetic. At one point, she was giving herself a dozen insulin shots per day, and on multiple occasions she had to be rushed to the hospital. One night, her mother Lori recalled in Memphis' *Commercial Appeal* in November 2007, "Grace awoke and was seriously sick. She had to sit and scoot down the staircase to wake us. We immediately went to the hospital. If she hadn't woken up that night, she could have easily died."

Through a nonprofit organization in Kansas called CARES (Canine Assistance Rehabilitation Education and Services), the Hankses purchased a Labrador retriever named Garbo. The dog first learned obedience skills while working with an inmate in a Kansas prison, then learned scent discrimination skills from an experienced trainer. Finally, the CARES staff invited the Hanks family to Kansas to meet Garbo.

Grace herself had to continue to reinforce Garbo's diabetic-alert behavior, giving her a treat when her blood sugar was out of range. The training and reward system worked. Soon, Garbo was waking up Grace by licking her face when she scented that her blood sugar was low. Garbo accompanied Grace to school and everywhere else.

Dogs like Garbo cannot cure their owner's diabetes, but they can prevent seizures and, thus, damage to the body. In addition, they give everyone in the family some much-needed peace of mind. "With Garbo," Lori's mother says, "I feel safe going to bed at night."

PART VI
Getting Around
The Unstoppable Traveler

Chapter Twenty-One

Run, Rhonda, Run!

Power to Run Fast

Pat C Rendezvous, the fastest greyhound in the world, waited anxiously for the gates to open so she could catch the mechanical bunny. Rain was falling at the Palm Beach Kennel Club track on that spring day in 1994, but fans packed the stands to see if "Rhonda" (Pat C Rendezvous' nickname) would win her thirty-third consecutive race, which would set an unofficial world record. They waved banners that read "Help, Help Me Rhonda" and "Pat C Rendezvous for President."

Finally, the gates opened and the dogs blasted down the track. For decades, dog lovers have protested the morality of greyhound racing, but the breathtaking speed of the magnificent animals (and, yes, the gambling that accompanies the sport) continues to mesmerize spectators. Despite a muddy surface, Rhonda zoomed around the track at a speed no human could approach. She completed the 3/8ths-of-a-mile race in just 38.47 seconds—seven lengths, incidentally, ahead of No. 2 finisher Mr. Pushups. All hailed Rhonda, the fastest dog in the world.

Greyhounds, of course, are not the only speedy breed of canines. Even little cockapoos, while chasing squirrels, yank their owners with their leashes because the latter are too slow to keep up. When we look down at our four-legged friends, many of whom don't even reach our knees, we ask in bewilderment: How can such little dogs run so darned fast?

Some of the reasons are obvious. As quadrupedal animals (as opposed to bipedal animals like humans), dogs have four limbs that can propel them forward. They also don't have to lug 190 pounds (the weight of the average American man) when they're scampering down the block. Moreover, their large hearts and lungs (compared to humans') help them send oxygen-rich blood to their muscles, which allows their muscles to perform at a higher level than humans'. A dog's heart can actually beat more than 270 times per minute—nearly twice the rate of humans.

A dog's oxygen intake actually coincides perfectly with its gallop. When a dog extends its rear legs, it exhales heavily. When it pushes the back legs forward, it inhales a great deal of air. Back legs back (air out), back legs forward (air in). This keeps the oxygen flowing, the blood pumping, and the legs moving.

A dog's speed depends on its girth and the length of its body and legs. Those with short legs, such as corgis and dachshunds, are slowpokes compared to long-bodied, long-legged dogs. Greyhounds not only fit that profile, but they also have three other traits that make them extraordinarily fast. First, their level of red blood cells is higher than that of other breeds, which allows them to send an even greater amount of oxygen to the muscles than other dogs. Moreover, the breed's hindquarters are especially muscular and powerful.

Also, a greyhound (and a few other breeds, including the deerhound and the saluki) runs with a "double suspension gallop." He launches his run with his back legs, but instead of landing on his back legs or on all fours, his front paws grab the ground and propel him forward. Explain dog experts Raymond and Lorna Coppinger, co-authors of the 2001 book *Dogs: A Startling New Understanding of Canine Origin, Behavior & Evolution,* "An animal that is really fast doesn't spend very much time floating around the air, but keeps the leg levers pulling and pushing against the earth, constantly overcoming gravity and catapulting the body forward."

Greyhounds have captivated humans for millennia. The only breed of dog mentioned in the Bible, they served as hunting dogs for centuries, chasing down such animals as deer and wild boar. Beginning in the 1920s, greyhound racing became popular in the United States. To this day, gamblers in the U.S., the United Kingdom, and Australia watch the dogs whiz around the track while chasing energized bunnies. Animal rights activists claim the dogs are not properly cared for and that too many of them are euthanized after their racing careers are over. Nevertheless, fans continue to support the sport.

Greyhounds run 35 to 40 mph in dog races, and a select few have reached 45 on the speed gun. This puts them in the same class as race-horses. Thoroughbreds average 38 mph at the Kentucky Derby, while quarter horses can approach 50 mph over short distances. Greyhounds also make the list of the fastest animals on earth. Only the cheetah (70 mph) and pronghorn antelope (60) are considerably faster, although other animals (lion, elk, gazelle, etc.) run in the 40-to 50-mph range.

Another breed of dogs, the saluki, has impressed humans with its breathtaking speed for thousands of years. The Egyptians, in fact, mummified these revered creatures. Built like greyhounds, they are identified by the feathery hair on their ears. It is difficult to precisely determine a saluki's speed, since the animal has no interest in racing or chasing mechanical rabbits. But experts put the saluki's top speed at 35 mph—maybe higher. Salukis are also able to sustain their great speed for great distances. Long ago, salukis who were trained for hunting chased down desert gazelles, who could run 50 mph but didn't have the salukis' stamina.

Finally, we end with the tragic story of a man who tried to run as fast as his dog. In the early 1920s, C. Curtis Woodruff was a star sprinter on Cornell University's track team. After graduation, he joined his father's contracting business in Long Island, New York. One day after work in 1926, on a particularly warm spring evening, Woodruff decided to play with his dog. Spot darted behind a lilac bush and then began racing around the house. Woodruff chased after him, chugging as hard as he could, but Spot was just too fast.

An hour later, Woodruff's father found his son lying on the garage floor, dead. According to *Time* magazine, "the run had been too much for his heart." The moral of the story is clear: No man, no matter how hard he tries, is as fast as the family dog.

Chapter Twenty-Two

Top of the World

Power to Climb Mountains

As five climbers began to ascend Mt. Aconcagua in 1995, they spotted a stray dog that wanted to tag along. They didn't discourage the pooch, figuring eventually he would turn around and retreat down the mountain. After all, the poor dog couldn't possibly follow them all the way up the 23,000-foot mountain in South America's Andes range. Or could he?

Outside of the Himalayas, Mt. Aconcagua is the tallest mountain in the world, and many people have died in their quest to reach the summit. Yet the hearty dog kept following the experienced climbers. Eventually the dog wandered off, and mountain guide Armin Liedl thought he'd never see him again. But one morning, he showed up next to Liedl's tent, shivering.

"Then I decided to climb with him up to the peak," Liedl says, "and if we made it, to call him Summit."

The dog not only climbed four miles into the sky, but at 21,000 feet he proved heroic. The courageous canine noticed two Argentine climbers who were lost and suffering from altitude sickness. The dog barked to alert Liedl and his fellow climbers, who went to help the ailing men.

Despite the slippery, steep terrain, the dog climbed all the way to the peak. He had conquered Mt. Aconcagua with nothing more than four paws and sheer will.

For those who want to write off "Summit" as a one-hit wonder, consider the case of Horton, an English Labrador retriever from Breckenridge, Colorado. Instead of going for a walk around the block, Horton goes for a hike up the mountain. In August 2008, Ronda Scholting reported that the mighty canine has ascended 14,000-foot Quandary Peak all by himself—sometimes several times a day! According to his owner, David Pfau, the dog has reached the top 1,500 times.

"Horton knows this trail better than anybody," Pfau says. "It's really a Quandary thing. He's in love with this mountain."

At any point in the year, Horton likes to follow strangers to the top of Quandary. He even accompanies skiers and snow-boarders, for he loves to romp in the snow. On at least three occasions, he has saved people's lives—once leading a poor soul down the mountain during a blinding snowstorm.

So the question remains: How does a dog—with no map, equipment, shoes, or clothes—climb as well as an experienced, well-equipped human mountain climber?

The answer says more about us than about dogs. As bipedal creatures (rare among mammals), we are not born to ascend steep inclines. We walk on our two rear limbs, so when we ascend a hill or a mountain, we don't have the balance and stability of a quadruped.

Dogs, though, are built to climb. Unlike humans' bare feet, dogs' paws are hard enough to walk on rough terrain. The paws also provide traction and shock absorption. With four limbs of equal ability and with relatively short legs, dogs are able to maintain extraordinary balance. In fact, their anatomies are similar to those of the greatest mountain-climbing animals on earth, such as mountain lions and snow leopards.

Of course, it's one thing to ascend a short, steep incline; it's another to climb a 14,000-foot mountain, like Horton. To do so requires tremendous strength and stamina, and some breeds of dogs have an ample supply of both. Granted, a teacup poodle can barely pull its own shadow. But other breeds are phenomenally strong. An Alaskan malamute, for example, can pull more than three thousand pounds on wheels. Certainly, then, dogs have the strength to haul their small butts up a mountain.

As for stamina, dogs' heavily oxygenated blood helps their muscles perform extremely well—meaning great strength and stamina. Each year, dogs prove their stamina in the Iditarod Trail Sled Dog Race, traveling 1,161 miles in as little as nine days—and that's on snow in subzero weather.

Humans do have one advantage over dogs: We can ascend vertically because, as primates, we can use our forelimbs to hoist ourselves up. Just like a monkey grabs branches on a tree to go higher and higher, we can grab rocks or pull ourselves on a rope to ascend higher. No dogs can do that...or can they?

Besides mountains, dogs can actually climb a wide variety of things, including fences, ladders, and even trees. In Washington, Illinois, a dog named Cody often ascends a blue spruce to get a closer look at the birds. The dog's owner, Pat Tully, has seen her climb forty feet up the tree. "I couldn't stop her from doing it if I wanted to, so it's like it's meant to be," Tully says. "Literally, every day, any kind of weather, she'll be up in these trees."

Of course, dogs are not invincible when they climb mountains or "hike" on rough terrain. They can fall victim to thirst, hunger, overheating, and extreme cold. They can take a bad tumble or hurt themselves in other ways. Their pads can get worn down and become sore, and an out-of-shape dog may not have the needed stamina. Dogs also can get lost, and the stream water that they drink might not be good for them.

In general, veterinarians say, dogs should stay away from mountains. Notes Portland vet Julie Kittams, "Any sport that requires safety gear, like harnesses, crampons, ice axes, and rope, is probably not an appropriate place for a pet dog to be."

Kittams is probably right. Still, she'd have a hard time convincing Rupee. Once a homeless dog who was found starving in a dump in India, Rupee was nursed back to health by his owner, Joanne Lefson. In 2013, Rupee climaxed his comeback by ascending Mount Everest. Along with Lefson, he trekked for ten days to base camp, 17,000 feet above sea level. He was believed to be the first dog ever to reach that height.

Chapter Twenty-Three

Like a Fish in Water

Power to Swim Naturally

Santos seemed like a spoiled little rich dog. A playful, black-haired schipperke, his "job" was to keep the Muilenburg family company during their frequent sailing excursions along the Caribbean and the coast of South Africa. Little did Peter and Dorothy Muilenberg know that their cute companion was blessed with special powers.

The schipperke, whose name means "little captain," was formed as a breed in the 1880s. In Belgium, schipperkes became known as extraordinary water dogs. While traveling aboard horse-pulled barges in canals, their job was to periodically get into the water and nip at the heels of the horses to get them moving. Schipperkes, the canal workers understood, were outstanding little swimmers.

Santos discovered his swimming powers before he was three months old. Twice falling off a boat, he treaded water briefly until he was saved. But as a full-grown dog in 1991, Santos endured a much more harrowing experience. Sailing on the family boat five miles off the Venezuelan coast, he fell overboard at nighttime while the Muilenburgs were sleeping. Not until Dorothy and Peter reached shore the next morning did they realize that their dog was nowhere to be found. Oh no, they realized, Santos had drowned at sea.

But not so fast. Later that morning, a port captain shouted excitedly to the grieving couple. "You won't believe it," he cried. "I just called the fishing boats on the radio...and the last boat said they caught nothing—except a little black dog!" Santos, a descendant of the Belgian canal dogs, had treaded water throughout the night.

Most breeds of dogs are natural swimmers. Yes, they might freak out and "freeze" when they venture into water for the first time, but many learn to swim very quickly. First of all, dogs in general are somewhat (but not completely) buoyant in the water, just like humans. And as with people, dogs with more body fat are more buoyant, because fat is less dense than bone and muscle.

Instinctively, dogs know to paddle all four paws at once and keep their heads above water. The paddling motion is so instinctive that some dogs actually start paddling when their owners hold them above a bathtub—or, as *America's Funniest Videos* revealed—above a toilet. Some dogs learn to swim even better if properly trained. You can train a dog to swim by tossing them a toy to fetch or rewarding them for swimming to you.

Some breeds of dogs swim like fish. In fact, water spaniels and the Portuguese water dog love to swim as much as most dogs love to run. In general, sporting breeds love outdoor activities, including running and swimming. These include various spaniels, setters, and retrievers. Labrador retrievers may be the best-known canine swimmers. The labs' swimming skills, great strength, and retriever instincts have made them heroic in the water. Small-town newspapers have been filled with stories of Labradors rescuing people who were about to drown.

In May 2006 in Colorado, Zion—a two-year-old yellow Lab—was enjoying fetching sticks thrown into the Roaring Fork River by his owner, Chelsea Bennett. Suddenly, Zion spotted an eight-year-old boy, Ryan Rambo, who had fallen off a raft. Noticing the child drifting helplessly downstream, Zion swam to him and then transported him to the riverbank.

Newfoundlands continue to amaze us with their water skills. Named after the Canadian province that juts into the Atlantic Ocean, Newfies used to accompany fishermen to work each day. The large, powerful dogs hauled nets into the sea and then yanked them back to the boat. They, too, have saved many men, women, and children from drowning. Due to their thick undercoats and oily outer coats, Newfoundlands can swim in cold water for hours.

Not all breeds of dogs can swim. Bulldogs, with their heavy bodies and short legs, don't stand much of a chance in the water. Marjorie Kelley found that out the hard way. When her bulldog jumped into a shallow creek, "she literally sank," Kelley recalls. "I've never seen anything like it. She sank like a bowling ball and didn't even move her legs to try and do the doggie paddle; she just wailed her head back and forth."

Not just "bowling ball" dogs struggle in the water. So do breeds with low body fat, such as boxers, greyhounds, and Doberman pinschers. Wendy Diamond, editorial director of *Animal Fair* magazine, says that basset hounds, corgis, dachshunds, pugs, and Scottish and Boston terriers are poor swimmers.

Older dogs and those with physical problems may also have trouble in the water. "No matter how well a dog can swim under supervision, any dog can drown," says Georgia Molek, a veterinarian with the American Animal Hospital Association. "All dogs can get fatigued, too, and/or become disoriented."

Small breeds of dogs may get cold quickly in chilly water, and most dogs struggle when the current or waves are too strong. For these reasons, boaters should consider life jackets for their dogs to avoid Santos-like situations. Dogs can swim just as well in pools as in natural bodies of water *except* when it comes to an exit strategy. Dogs cannot easily climb ladders or pull themselves out of pools.

While most dogs paddle slowly, some can motor at a fast pace for a long distance. Take Umbra, who Guinness World Records recognized as the fastest long-distance dog swimmer in the world. As a two-year-old in 1992, Umbra (of unknown breeds) swam a mile in 28.5

minutes. Another time, she swam 5.5 miles in two hours.

Umbra became such a celebrity that in 1997 the Turkish Olympic Committee invited her to compete in a field of outstanding human swimmers. Out of approximately two hundred competitors in a 4.3-mile race, she finished with a faster time than 80 percent of them. To this day she is still revered as Umbra the Wonder Dog.

PART VII
What Comes Naturally
Dogs on Autopilot

Chapter Twenty-Four

Did You Hear the One About...

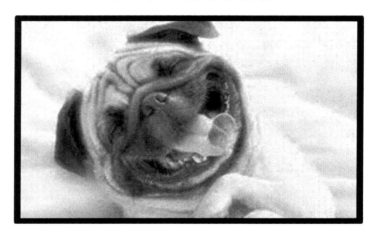

Power to Laugh

Your goldendoodle may be laughing behind your back.

No, she's not laughing *at* you; dogs aren't that mean. But she is definitely capable of laughing when she is happy and excited. So said Patricia Simonet, an animal behaviorist who pioneered the exploration of dog laughter before her death in 2011 at age 51.

Simonet's team of researchers studied dogs at play in a park. With the use of a parabolic microphone, they were able to record all the sounds that the dogs emitted. Simonet found that the pant a dog makes when it's simply hot or tired is much different than the pant it elicits when it's at play. "To an untrained human ear, [the playful pant] sounds much like [the hot or tired] pant:

'hhuh, hhuh,'" Simonet said. But it's actually different. The playful dog pant, she discovered in her recordings, has a much broader range of frequencies.

In the next phase of her study, Simonet played the recording of these joyful pants, which she called laughter, for other dogs to hear. Such sounds made the dogs pick up toys and play by themselves.

Eventually, Simonet's findings were put to good, practical use. She created a CD of dog laughter that was played at the Spokane (Washington) County Regional Animal Protection Service, a dog shelter known as SCRAPS. By listening to the CD, the dogs' stress behaviors—such as pacing, growling, and cowering—were significantly reduced. "Some sounds, like growls, confused the puppies," Simonet said. "But the dog laugh caused sheer joy and brought down the stress levels in the shelter immediately."

In fact, the CD sounds were found to increase tail wagging, make the dogs more in the mood for play, and increase their pro-social behavior with people. As such, they became more appealing to shelter visitors and were thus more likely to be adopted.

In recent years, scientists have come to the consensus that laughter is common throughout the animal kingdom. We people just hadn't realized it because we didn't see animals chuckling and giggling and doubling over like we do. Animals laugh in different ways.

Jaak Panksepp, a neuroscientist with Bowling Green State University, discovered joy among the rat community. Panksepp had been studying rat vocalizations for years before he decided to test for laughter. "I went to the lab and tickled some rats," he told the *Chicago Tribune*. "Tickled them gently around the nape of their necks. Wow!"

He discovered that tickling made the rats chirp joyfully, but only "as long as the animal's friendly toward you," he said. "If not, you won't get a single chirp, just like a child that might be suspicious of an adult."

Panksepp told the *Tribune* that "neural circuits for laughter exist in very ancient regions of the brain, and ancestral forms of play and laughter existed in other animals eons before we humans came along."

Laughter is certainly common among chimpanzees. They may not chuckle when we dress them up in Blues Brothers suits, but they laugh when they roughhouse with one another and when they're tickled. Their laughter is different than humans because of their anatomy.

"We humans laugh on outward breaths," psychologist and neuroscientist Robert Provine told the *Chicago Tribune*. "When we say 'ha-ha-ha,' we're chopping an outward breath. Chimps can't do that. They make one sound per inward and outward breath. They don't have the breath control to...make the traditional human laugh."

If a chimpanzee, our closest relative in the animal kingdom, cannot laugh like us, then a dog certainly can't do so. Instead it laughs in its own way, with sounds at frequencies we cannot hear unless we have the equipment that Patricia Simonet used.

Before her passing, Simonet taught us how to share laughter with our dogs "If you want to invite your dog to play using the dog laugh, say 'hee, hee, hee' without pronouncing the 'ee,'" Simonet said. "Force out the air in a burst, as if you're receiving the Heimlich maneuver."

Stanley Coren, the famed "dog psychologist," says that producing dog laughter correctly "can make your dog sit up, wag his tail, approach you from across the room, and even laugh along." He offers his own advice on how to make a dog laugh, which is slightly different than Simonet's recommendation. Coren advices: 1) Round your lips slightly to make a 'hhuh' sound. Note: The sound has to be breathy with no actual voicing, meaning that if you touch your throat while making this sound, you should not feel any vibration. 2) Use an open-mouthed smiling expression to make a 'hhah' sound. Again, breathe the sound; do not voice it. 3) Combine steps one and two to create canine laughter. It should sound like 'hhuh-hhah-hhuh-hhah.'"

When your dog starts panting and playing and wagging its tail, you know you've got a happy, laughing pooch.

Not only do dogs "laugh," they also have a sense of humor. So says Jane "Dr. Barkman" Brackman, an authority on canine biology. In a 2013 blog, Brackman told the story of a friend of hers who used a guide dog. The friend told her: "My dog would confidently guide me to the wrong hotel room door, always the one that was just before ours. I knew this was a joke and not pure naughtiness because she would wag her tail furiously and make a happy dog laughing-huffing sound, then take me to the correct door. She loved playing this game and would wag even more furiously when we finally arrived at the correct room, as if to say, 'Wasn't that just the funniest thing?'"

Hilarious

Chapter Twenty-Five

Sit! Sitz! Sientate!

Power to Learn in Multiple Languages

Some dogs may be hard to train, but at least it doesn't matter what language you're speaking. All human languages sound the same to a dog, so it's easy to teach even old dogs new languages.

Take business owners and entrepreneurs of various stripes; they don't hesitate to take advantage of their multicultural pets. In Wengen, Switzerland, hotel owner Christian Straessle realized the cash-in potential of his multilingual mutt, who he regally named General Sam Houston Jr., or Housty for short. By the age of two, Housty responded to commands in German, French, English, Spanish, and Japanese. Straessle's international clientele paid good money to go on outings with Housty, and at one point, there was a waiting list fifty people long just to take Housty on a walk.

But even Housty is no match for the late, great Jim the Wonder Dog, who at one time drew international fame to a small Midwestern town. Jim, a black and white English setter, was born in 1927. His owner, Sam Van Arsdale, realized Jim's potential during a routine hunting foray in the fields near Sedalia, Missouri. Van Arsdale recalled that he casually told Jim they needed to "sit in the shade of that hickory tree and rest." As if the request had been understood, Jim trotted over to the nearby hickory tree.

Van Arsdale wondered what else his dog was capable of. He asked Jim to show him an oak tree, and Jim trotted over to the nearest oak. From that day onward, Van Arsdale trained Jim to do a variety of tricks, including how to respond to commands in Italian, French, German, and Spanish. Jim created such a sensation that a group of veterinarians and research scientists at the University of Missouri examined him. They reported that, physically, Jim was a normal dog, yet he could indeed respond accurately to requests in multiple languages.

Many concluded that Jim was a dog of inexplicable intelligence and power. Van Arsdale was convinced Jim was a gift from God: In 1932, Disney offered Van Arsdale $364,000 to make a movie about Jim, but Van Arsdale declined, thinking it would be wrong to profit from divine gifts. Yet while Jim's feats were unusual and some remain unexplained to this day, there is nothing supernatural about a dog that learns commands in multiple languages. It is likely that Jim the Wonder Dog was responding more to intonation and body language than anything else.

Dogs and humans have evolved starkly different systems of communication, and a dog is no more sensitive to the nuances of human speech than humans are to the nuances of doggie body language. Dogs, like most mammals, depend a good deal on body language and facial expression to understand one another. Humanity's added repertoire of words, and the countless layers of meaning allowed by them, is a unique trait. The brainpower required for language is responsible for the fact that humans have the greatest brain to body size ratio of any species that has ever existed.

Dogs, meanwhile, have canine brains, and while they can surely pick up on the pitch, volume, and intonation of a given command, they would not notice if the language was different. What they *would* notice are the various elements of communication that dogs recognize in their simpler form of vocal communication with one another.

In 2003, scientists at the University of California, Davis, recorded more than 4,672 barks from ten adult dogs. The two head researchers, Sophia Yin and Brenda McCowan, concluded that barks differ in terms of frequency, intonation, and length of pauses between barks. The kind of bark delivered was easily predictable, based on the situation the barker was in. In their final report on the experiment, McCowan and Yin explain that "the harsh, low-frequency, unmodulated barks were more commonly given in the disturbance situation, and the more tonal, higher-pitch, modulated barks were more commonly given in the isolation and play situations."

McCowan and Yin's findings fall exactly in line with a general rule called Morton's rule, which seems to apply to all canines and possibly all mammals. The simplified version is: low-pitched sounds are associated with aggression, and high pitched sounds are associated with affection or "help-solicitation," which might translate as, "Come here! I need help!" Animals mix the pitches to get across shades of meaning.

Pitch and frequency also have an effect on the animal that hears the sound. A rapid succession of high-pitched sounds (the "help me!" scenario) causes increased blood pressure in the listener, who is induced to track down the possibly fallen comrade. Low-pitched, aggressive sounds can elicit the flight-or-fight response in the listener. Sensitivity to these auditory cues crosses species lines. A dog knows its master is saying something harsh or threatening, even if the specific content of the words is not understood.

Dogs may also be able to interpret the body language of their masters. For a dog, a long stare always means "I'm challenging you!" Whoever looks away first has admitted defeat. A lowered head and body is also sign of submission, while forward-arching, stiff bodies are signs of aggression or domination. Most dog owners recognize the signature "Let's play!" gesture—rear in the air and forebody lowered, this is a staple combination of dominant and submissive poses.

When dogs respond to human commands, they are probably responding to body language and voice intonation. Dog trainer John Ross believes these two elements must be consistent with each command. In his book *Dog Talk: Training Your Dog Through a Canine Point of View,* Ross recommends that "the tone of voice when issuing the command should be crisp and authoritative...the command word should be accompanied by a slight 'correction' or signal by hand or by touch." Ross adds that trainers must take the same approach when it comes to positive reinforcement, asserting that "lavish praise along with the happy high voice and lots of hugs and kisses is without a doubt the most desired reward on the part of the dog."

So whether a dog hears Sit!, *Sientate!* (Spanish), *Assis!* (French), *Seduto!* (Italian), or *Sitz!* (German), what the dog really "hears" is tone and body language. Though dogs are not by definition multilingual, their ability to follow orders is remarkable just the same.

Chapter Twenty-Six

A Lot to Swallow

Power to Ingest Foreign Objects

X-rays don't lie. Ask any veterinarian, and he or she likely will have at least a few tales—and perhaps even some visual black-and-white evidence—about dogs that turned everyday objects into unhealthy, indigestible, and sometimes unfathomable meals.

Silverware is commonly found in dogs' stomachs. Countless articles of clothing have made their way into the belly of the beast. A plastic squirrel figurine was among the more unusual sights one vet saw and removed. A dog in the Houston area ingested the blade of a large electric knife. Dr. Brian Poteet of Gulf Coast Veterinary Specialists kept the X-ray from that one, perhaps out of disbelief.

"Why a dog would eat that, I'm not sure," he says. "But we try to figure out that question a lot."

The answer to why dogs swallow foreign objects might never be known. One theory traces the behavior back to their hunting ancestors—beasts that would kill for food and consume the entire carcass, bones and all. Solid objects, in this theory, constitute modern-day roughage in their diet.

A more common theory points to a dog's love for chewing things, or exploring with their mouths. Chewing, which can be good for dogs' teeth, is a common canine behavior. The objects being chewed must be either spit out or swallowed. Unfortunately, many dogs seem to prefer the latter, even though it can endanger their health and their very lives.

A thirteen-pound Lhasa apso swallowed a rubber ball that remained in the dog's stomach for more than ten years. More typically, frequent vomiting alerts owners to a problem in the hours after ingestion, though it is not uncommon for foreign objects to remain in the digestive system for weeks or months before being passed or discovered.

And sometimes, the evidence is right there, hanging out of the pooch's mouth. "One of my clients got a puppy who ate rocks and swallowed whole socks," exclaims certified dog behavior consultant Lynn Hoover, noting that the dog was a Labrador retriever, "known for their ravenous appetites and non-discriminative tastes."

"One day," Hoover continues, "they returned home to find the crate door open—they must not have latched it properly. There he was, their Labrador, with something unusual hanging from his mouth. It turned out he'd ingested a panty hose. One leg had gone down the throat; the other leg was waving about. My clients pulled...and pulled some more...until they got their panty hose back, which was too disgusting to use again.

"The pup wagged his tail, let out a 'woof,' and set off looking for his next 'meal,' without shame."

Studies of the most popular nonfood items consumed by dogs consistently place panty hose and underwear among the most common. Other items ranking high on those lists are sticks, socks, rocks, balls, chew toys, corn cobs, bones, and any number of hair items, such as ties, bows, and ribbons. However, some dogs seem to have no limit to the size and nature of what seems like a meal. Lost pagers and cell phones have been found inside four-legged "containers." A young golden retriever chewed up and swallowed a brand new, expensive 35-mm camera.

While these stories can be humorous once the objects are passed or retrieved and the animal moves on to its next adventure, instances of sticks, stones, string, fishing lures, and any number of items being swallowed by dogs can be life-threatening. Vets urge owners to limit dogs' access to such items. They also emphasize the importance of recognizing the warning signs that one's dog might have used its powerful teeth and strong constitution to swallow an indigestible object.

If the item is stuck in the mouth, there may

be bleeding, excessive drooling, or signs of the dog pawing at the mouth in an effort to free it. Should an object become lodged in the throat, choking and gagging is common, as the dog may be struggling to breathe. In those cases, owners can frequently pry out or dislodge the obstruction on their own.

When an item reaches the stomach or intestines, frequent vomiting is the most common symptom. Dry, sunken eyes or loss of skin elasticity can be signs of dehydration in these cases. Large items might even be felt in the stomach region. These signs are cues to see a veterinarian immediately. X-rays can diagnose the problem. Frequently, the items can be removed with an endoscope—a tool with a tiny camera and grasping mechanism that is inserted through the mouth. In other cases, surgery might be required to prevent damage to the intestines, small bowel, or other vital organs.

And in some cases, the vets simply have to shake their heads and laugh after the successful removal of such items. One terrier mistook a ten-inch steel tent peg for a bone and swallowed it. It was successfully recovered after an X-ray. A Yorkshire terrier felt much better after having eight balloons removed from her stomach. And one particular bull mastiff, in a one-year span, had a TV remote control and more than twenty pairs of underwear removed from his stomach, some almost fully intact.

Christmas ornaments, light bulbs, shoes, books...there seems to be no end to what a dog can pass through its esophagus.

"People go to great lengths to child-proof

their homes," says Dr. Sheila McCullough of the University of Illinois Veterinary Teaching Hospital. "It would save people a lot of grief and money if they would pet-proof their homes as well.... If they can get into it, they will."

And if they can get into it, there's a good chance it can get into them. X-rays don't lie.

Chapter Twenty-Seven

Joie de Vie

Power to Maintain
a Zest for Life

Waffle, a slightly hefty cockapoo, was a typical Chicago dog. If he could talk he'd say something like "d'ose guys" who chow down at Mr. Beef, barhop in Wrigleyville, and cheer on "da Bears," Waffle had an I-don't-give-a-poop personality and a desire to enjoy the day.

This buff-colored chunkaroo lived on the first floor of a condo building, but that didn't hold her back. As a puppy, she loved to romp in the park with her German shepherd friend, Rusty. Waffle would hold on to the big dog's leash, and Rusty would take off, taking his thrill-seeking friend on a fastbreak joyride. By nighttime, Waffle still had enough energy for a game of dogball in the condo's narrow hallway. The object of the game was to kick the tennis ball past the pooch, who defended her goal like hockey's Martin Brodeur.

Waffle, of course, loved to eat. If you left a McDonald's cheeseburger within her reach, a minute later there'd be nothing left but the wrapper and a pickle. Each day, Waffle—on her own—climbed to the third floor to say hi to Katherine, leaving only after a tummy rub and a satisfying snack. At Grandma's, Waffle buddied up with a schnauzer named Leasel. Together they would share the cats' dry food, with Waffle grabbing the nuggets from the bowl and giving them to her canine pal.

Waffle may have had her own quirks, but in essence she was no different than every other dog. From Airedales to yorkipoos, dogs have a genuine zest for life. It starts from the moment they awake. After a quick stretch, they're pawing at our beds, ready for a morning trot and a hearty breakfast. "I could really go for a large can of beef," they seem to be thinking at 6:30 in the morning, "or a turkey dinner with all the fixin's." By contrast, we're sipping coffee two hours later, still trying to wake up.

Even compared to other animals (scurrying rodents notwithstanding), dogs seem especially peppy. The next time you visit the zoo, count the number of gorillas, elephants, lions, goats, and giraffes that run up to you, tails wagging. On a visit to a farm, you might get a tilt of the head from a cow or a horse, but nothing more—unless the farmer's dog blasts open the screen door and runs to greet you.

In *Living with Dogs,* J. Allen Boone describes the sheer joy a dog experiences in a simple game of fetch: "'Throw it again,' the dog asks in no uncertain terms. A Frisbee, a ball, a stick: Dog doesn't care about what's thrown, only about the throwing, the joyous silky flow of living the moment."

"Dogs are famous for their undying enthusiasm for life," effuses Audrey Pavia, author of *The Labrador Retriever Handbook*. "They relish in simple pleasures: eating, sleeping, and playing. No matter what is going on in the world, dogs are always optimistic. They have an innate joy that is truly inspiring."

Dogs' zestfulness can be partially explained. Let's start with the greeting at the door. As we all know, dogs go bonkers when a family member comes home—wagging their tails, jumping for joy, licking their owners' faces. Veterinarians tie this behavior to the dogs' pack mentality. Like the wolves from which they descend, dogs only feel "whole" when the pack members are together. "What we call family," states Jim Mathys of Quality K-9 Services, "your dog sees as his pack."

While alone in the house, the dog is anything but zestful. He will mope, sleep, or stare out the window for hours waiting for you to return. He is a lone wolf, incomplete and sad. But when you come home—when the pack is back—he is instantly full of life. He is especially glad to see his caregivers, meaning those who provide him with food, affection, exercise, security—everything he needs to survive and enjoy life.

Sometimes, however, we misperceive what we think is zestful behavior. In other words, when we see our bichon running at a breakneck pace for a squeaky toy, she may *seem* like she's on an adrenaline rush but she is actually operating at a normal pace. With their blood rich in oxygen, dogs' muscles are able to perform at a high level. Dogs can run fast, dart quickly, and maintain their stamina for a long time. For them, it's all rather ordinary.

What we perceive as a dog's zestful *personality* may say more about us than the pooch. Dogs have simple minds and lives. They like to play with toys, run around, be coddled, interact with others, and pay attention to interesting sights, sounds, and smells. In this respect, they are very much like happy toddlers. (According to Dr. Stanley Coren, an expert on dog intelligence, a dog's cognitive ability is roughly the same as a two- or three-year-old child's.)

Compared to grown-ups, dogs and toddlers may have more zest because their minds and lives are simpler. They are not preoccupied and burdened with homework, housework, peer pressure, money worries, work issues, relationship problems, and all the other negative and complicated thoughts that clutter our minds. It is not surprising that people have more zest when they're on a worry-free vacation. Vacationers are happier when they get to sleep in, frolic in the water, and play with golf and tennis balls—in other words, when they get to live more like dogs.

Although dogs lose some of their pep as they get older, most of them maintain their positive attitude. Even dogs with disabilities often surprise us with their zest. "My parents have a dog that is particularly full of life, despite many challenges," Pavia writes. Her parents own a tiny Pomeranian, Monique, who has canine epilepsy and suffers from seizures. But, Pavia insists, "in between her convulsions, you would never know anything was wrong with her. Always full of energy and happy to see everyone, she runs from person to person, lavishing each one with kisses. She races from one end of the room to the other with sheer joy, oblivious to the fact that she could begin seizing at any minute. That doesn't matter."

"Like all dogs," Pavia says, "she lives in the moment."

PART VIII
On the Job
Working for a Living

Chapter Twenty-Eight

Drug Detectors

Power to Sniff Out Contraband

Law enforcement agencies use a dog's extraordinary sense of smell for many purposes, but the most widespread use is drug detection. In fact, dogs are so good at sniffing out illegal substances that they sometimes get the job done even on their day off.

Dog trainer Ed Presnall is an expert in training dogs to track people, explosives, drugs, you name it. One day, Ed and his dog Race, a field spaniel, were sitting at the Houston airport, generally minding their own business and waiting for their flight to begin boarding. A group of males in their mid-twenties sat a few rows away.

Race had been trained in both drug detection and search-and-rescue missions. His current range of expertise was focused on search operations: as he sat in the airport, Race was wearing his SAR vest, proudly advertising his membership in this elite team of "Search and Rescue" dogs. But Race wasn't about to forget his duty in drug detection.

As Ed remembers it, Race suddenly "jumped down from his chair, skirted several rows of chairs, and approached the four men. Stopping in front of one of them, he placed his paw on a backpack sitting on the floor." Ed knew what this meant. He strolled over to the ticket counter and asked the agent to contact the local K9 ("canine") team—the drug detection dogs (usually called "sniffers") that frequent all major airports. The team promptly arrived, then arrested the four men just as Ed and Race boarded their plane.

Race certainly demonstrated the commitment of an off-duty dog, but in December 2007 a dog in the U.K. showed that even amateur dogs have powers of drug detection. A three-year-old pet dog was being walked by its owner in rural South Wales when the dog unearthed a substantial amount of amphetamines that had been hidden in the undergrowth. The drugs were worth almost a quarter-million dollars, and the local police considered it a major seizure.

In another well-publicized case, a dog named Tebow—named after heroic University of Florida quarterback Tim Tebow—fingered a drug smuggler at the Orlando International Airport. Weslie Morales faced serious prison time after Tebow sniffed the kilo of cocaine that was in the man's suitcase.

While dogs have been used to locate missing persons or dead bodies for millennia, their powerful role in drug detection is a recent phenomenon. The practice began in the 1960s and '70s, but really took off during the stepped-up "War on Drugs" in the '80s, '90s, and continuing into the twenty-first century. Since K9 teams are used by various law enforcement agencies, it's difficult to pinpoint exactly how many drug-sniffing canines are out there.

The numbers that are available point to the widespread and effective use of sniffers. In 2008, some four thousand law enforcement dog handlers claimed membership to the North American Police Work Dog Association, compared to one thousand members in 1994. During the past thirty years, sniffer dogs employed by U.S. Customs and other border-protection agencies have been directly responsible for a full 130,000 drug seizures.

Sniffer dogs are usually shepherds, bloodhounds, or beagles. They're trained for detection from mere puppyhood. Trainers keep an eye out for pups that have unusually high energy levels and an attitude of confidence and leadership within their litter. But most importantly, a future sniffer dog must love playing with its toys. From the beginning, training and playing are synonymous.

First, the trainer teaches the dog to play tug-of-war or hide-and-seek with a favorite toy—usually a towel. Next, the trainer rolls up a small amount of the drug substance within the towel, and hides it. The dog learns specific motions—such as pawing at the ground—to alert its trainer to the location of the "toy." Novice sniffer dogs realize that if they find the hidden toy, not only can the fun game continue but they are showered with lots of praise and affection. This routine is repeated with all kinds of drug-specific scents, and over time the sniffer dog alerts its trainer whenever it smells any type of drug.

Sniffer dogs are so good at their job that they often find themselves at the center of legal battles. The question "does a sniff constitute a search?" has been a crucial issue in legal cases that make it all the way to the Supreme Court. Since the Fourth Amendment to the U.S. Constitution protects individuals from being searched without a warrant or probable cause, any search set off by a dog's "sniff" would be illegal...but only if a sniff is a search.

In 1983, a Supreme Court decision upheld the rights of sniffer dogs to make random sniffs of luggage in airports. In 2005, the Supreme Court upheld the rights of sniffer dogs to have a go at it when cars are pulled over for routine traffic violations. Opponents of these decisions point out that a sniffer dog's indication of a drug does not constitute "probable cause," since probable cause assumes it is human police officers, and not dogs, who are supposed to perceive the likelihood of an illegal activity. Many are concerned that this particular dog power is strong enough to strip us humans of our rights and privacies.

The skills of sniffer dogs are indeed so coveted that a star sniffer dog was actually *cloned,* as part of an experiment to see if sniff-ability is mostly genetic. In 2007, scientists at Seoul National University in Seoul, South Korea, made seven copies of an adept, albeit deceased, sniffer dog. All of the puppies have already shown exceptional drug-sniffing ability. One of the puppies' trainers, Kim Nak-seung, described them as having "a superior nature. They are active and excel in accepting the training."

Sniffer dogs have also provided insight to scientists across the world who are harnessing nanotechnology to create sensitive smell-detectors. These sensors detect infinitesimally small concentrations of specific odorants, often in ways that imitate the efficient way that a dog's scent receptors signal specific smells to a dog's brain. Ironically, these smell-detecting machines might one day replace dogs as the world's best drug detectors.

So from drug raids to courtrooms to science labs, a dog's ability to detect drugs is one of both contention and inspiration. Regardless of what the future holds for K9 dogs, one thing is for certain—if you're hiding something illegal, you'd better hope there are no sniffers in the vicinity.

Chapter Twenty-Nine

Rover to the Rescue

Power to Locate
Disaster Victims

In New York City in 2001, the World Trade Center towers had collapsed just hours before, and members of New Jersey Task Force 1 of the U.S. Army Reserve arrived at Ground Zero—with their dogs. Shell-shocked firefighters, searching through the rubble for their dead brethren, perked up at the sight of a dozen search-and-rescue animals.

Sonny Whynman of NJ-TF1 recalls in *Dog Heroes of September 11th:* "There were dozens of firefighters and they were all pleading, 'Bring your search dog over here.'"

Sonny told his dog, Piper, to "go find," and the German shepherd went to work. Climbing over rough and jagged debris, Piper sniffed and sniffed in search of human beings. Unlike the human workers, the dogs worked without masks. They inhaled harmful smoke and their eyes turned red. Piper, like many of the other dogs, worked until his paws were bloody. All told, Piper and his canine teammates found about fifteen bodies. In a shelter that evening, after being treated and fed by appreciative volunteers, the dogs slept at their handlers' sides.

In every major disaster of recent decades—from 9/11 to the 2004 Indian Ocean tsunami, from Hurricane Andrew in 1992 to the earthquake in China in 2008—search-and-rescue dogs have answered the call of duty. Toiling for rewards, including praise and hugs, dogs have practically worked their tails off to save lives and discover remains.

In the wake of Hurricane Sandy, for example, a search dog named Jed went to Staten Island, New York. Jed and his handler conducted house-to-house searches looking for those who needed help. On the south side of Staten Island, Brutas searched for victims' bodies amid boats and debris washed ashore by the hurricane.

Not just any dog is suited for these difficult and often dangerous missions. Search-and-rescue (SAR) trainers usually select large-breed dogs that are physically gifted and have a strong sense of smell. German shepherds, golden retrievers, and Belgian Malinois are among the best-suited breeds for this line of work. Labrador retrievers excel at sniffing out cadavers, and Newfoundlands are dogs of choice during avalanche rescues.

Lazy, sluggish dogs will never make the cut. Trainers and handlers look for high-energy canines that love to play. Though their work is extremely serious and often grim, dogs see it as a complex game. SAR dogs are trained to follow a scent trail all the way to the end. When they reach that point, they are rewarded with praise, food, or perhaps tug-of-war with their favorite toy.

The dogs' ability to smell, of course, is extremely powerful—hundreds or thousands times stronger than humans. They also can detect many different scents with just once sniff. "We smell spaghetti cooking," says rescue dog trainer Carol Shapiro. "They smell basil, mushrooms, garlic. They can even smell who you slept with last night."

As SAR training progresses, the dog's searches become more complicated. Dogs can be trained to scent a generic human body, a cadaver, or—just by sniffing a piece of clothing—a particular person. During training for a disaster, one person often plays the part of the "body." For avalanche training, the "dying" person is forced to wait in a snow-covered pit until the dog arrives.

SAR dogs are trained in all kinds of weather. A dog needs to be able to perform in cold, rainy, and snowy conditions—each of which affect the scents. Avalanche rescue dogs endure particularly difficult training. These dogs learn to walk on slippery snow and ice, and they are trained to jump long and high. Their paws need to get used to the frozen tundra, and their eyes need to adjust to the blinding-white snow. They also have to work fast. "After half an hour, your chances are 50/50," says Brian Slusser, a ski patrol director in California's Sierra Mountains and the handler of a rescue dog. "That's why we have to get there as fast as possible."

Handlers work with the dogs on a regular basis to make sure the canines don't lose their edge. Besides natural disasters, certified SAR dogs can be called on for a variety of emergencies. Dogs are used to track down lost hikers and hunters as well as missing children and elderly Alzheimer's patients. They also search for survivors in burned or bombed-out buildings.

It takes a special type of animal to meet the SAR qualifications. In fact, there are fewer than two hundred U.S. government-certified rescue dogs. Jake was one such hero. A black Labrador, he was abandoned on a street with a broken leg and an injured hip as a puppy. "But against all odds, he became a world-class rescue dog," says his owner and handler, Mary Flood, a member of Utah Task Force 1.

Jake worked at Ground Zero on 9/11, searching for bodies despite breathing in toxic air. When Hurricane Katrina slammed the Gulf Coast, Flood and Jake drove from Utah to Mississippi to search for survivors in flooded homes. In his later years, Jake continued to serve, showing younger dogs how to track scents. They followed his lead as he sniffed scents in the snow and up the base of trees. In his down time, he visited the elderly at senior homes and brought comfort to burn victims in hospitals. When Jake died in July 2007, the national news media paid tribute to the fallen hero. Jake's ashes were scattered "in places that were important to him," says Flood, including the Utah training grounds and the hills he had once roamed.

After each natural disaster, stories inevitably emerge about heroic search-and-rescue dogs. During China's recent earthquake, one dog found fourteen students buried under a collapsed classroom. Also in China, a dog was so determined to recover a human victim that he stayed on task during an aftershock—and lost his life.

SAR handlers often speak reverently about their dogs, as if reminiscing about old war buddies who went beyond the call of duty. Sonny Whynman feels that way about Piper. "I have a partner who asks nothing of me except to stay at my side and do his work," Whynman says. "And when he's tired or hurting, he works even harder. In my next life, I would like to be that good."

—Chapter Thirty—
On Track

Power to Track People and Animals

Scott Peterson thought he would get away with murder. What he didn't count on was a four-legged "detective" named Trimble.

On Christmas Eve, 2002, Peterson killed his pregnant wife, Laci, and dumped her body in the marina in Berkeley, California. Scott, who reported his wife missing, told police that he had gone fishing at the marina that day and that when he returned home, Laci was missing.

Police were not convinced, so on December 28 they employed Eloise Anderson and her search dog, Trimble, to inspect the marina. Trimble, a Labrador retriever, sniffed Laci's sunglasses and then went to work. The highly trained dog picked up Laci's scent in the marina's parking lot. She followed the scent all the way to the dock area and then down a pier that ran along the boat launch. When she reached the end of the pier, Trimble sniffed over the water, where the trail obviously ended. The dog sat down, her work completed.

Anderson was convinced that Trimble had scented Laci's trail. "She pulled steady on the line, level head, and maintained that posture out to that pylon," Anderson recalls in the *San Francisco Chronicle*. "That's a behavior indicating she's working a valid scent trail."

Trimble's efforts indicated that Scott had *not* gone fishing by himself. Instead, it seemed likely that he had taken Laci, or her dead body, to the marina and pushed her off the pier. Among intense media scrutiny, Scott denied wrongdoing. But when Laci's body washed up on the marina's shoreline four months later, Scott—not Trimble—seemed like the "lying dog."

On August 31, 2004, Trimble's handler, Anderson, testified at Peterson's murder trial. Americans were amazed: How could a dog possibly pick up a person's scent *four days* after the person had walked the trail? But they can and do, even though researchers are not sure *how* they do it.

For decades, scientists have debated what exactly dogs follow when they track a person's scent. "Some claim that 'tracking' means the dog is following a 'track scent' or a cornucopia of crushed vegetation, decomposing earth, and disturbed earth created where we walk," writes Ed Presnall, who has worked with more than four thousand dogs in tracking. This theory, however, doesn't explain Trimble's success. After all, that dog traced Laci Peterson's scent not through crushed vegetation or "disturbed earth" but across a parking lot.

Presnall explains another theory: Some scientists believe that the dog follows human scent created by microscopic skin rafts (cells) that people continuously shed. Still others claim that tracking dogs follow both track scent and human scent. "My belief," Presnall writes, "is that the dog is following a combination of scents—ground, air, and skin rafts."

The "skin raft" theory seems plausible. According to Presnall, who authored the book *Mastering Variable Surface Tracking,* humans shed about 50 million cells each minute. These cells, when mixed with sweat and bacteria, have a distinct odor. "Rafts fall from the body," Presnall describes, "like a shower of tiny confetti for the dogs to follow."

Presnall writes that the rafts mix with the odor of the grass and disturbances of the ground from footsteps to make a "pattern" for the tracking dog to follow. "Like our DNA, each of our scent patterns is unique," Presnall points out. "Dogs detect these rafts, as well as other tracklayer scents, including breath and sweat vapor. Each person's scent trail is unique, and dogs are remarkably good at separating one person's trail from another's."

Presnall's insights explain how Trimble tracked Laci

Peterson's body. But how do search-and-rescue dogs find unknown people who are buried in snow due to an avalanche or in rubble because of an earthquake? Such animals are called "airscenting" dogs (as opposed to "trailing" dogs like Trimble). These dogs are trained to locate a generic human scent, and their powers are remarkable. Dogs have been known to detect human scents from more than a quarter-mile away. Many factors affect a dog's ability to airscent, including terrain, temperature, and humidity. German shepherds, golden retrievers, border collies, and Labradors are among the most talented airscenting canines.

The training of tracking and search-and-rescue dogs is intense, and in fact most dogs do not have the "right stuff"; most do not complete their training. Presnall tells the story of one young dog that did make it all the way through his training program. In order to pass his final exam, the dog had to trace a scent for more than a thousand yards. Luckily, a light drizzle had fallen that morning, enhancing the scenting conditions.

"Starting at the steps of a nursing home, we had wound our way across streets, down alleys, through the front and back yards of homes, and in and out of commercial areas," Presnall recalls. The dog turned down a dirt path between houses, but lost the scent. Not giving up, he retreated and picked up the scent again. He entered the gate of a yard and continued through a small park. "Weaving through the jungle gym and across the sandbox, he entered a parking lot," Presnall recalls. The dog moved so fast that Presnall lost sight of him. When he finally caught up with the power-scenting pooch, he found that the dog had reached his destination.

Presnall's colleague's rewarded the dog with treats. "A cookie from this one, a pet here, a belly rub there," Presnell describes. The dog had successfully completed the program. He would now be on call with the local search-and-rescue response team as an Urban Search Dog. "We'll wait for the phone call to say we are needed," Presnall insists, "and rush to the scene to utilize his special talents."

—Chapter Thirty-One—
Riding Herd

Power to Herd Livestock

During his trip to Uruguay in the 1820s, French explorer Alcide Dessalines d'Orbigny was astonished by the actions of a single dog. This super canine guarded and herded a flock of sheep without any supervision. Each evening, the dog rounded up the sheep and herded them into a corral, where he slept among them. Only at mealtime would the dog run to the farmhouse; otherwise, he ruled the flock.

For hundreds of years, humans and herding dogs have worked together to herd sheep, cattle, goats, and other animals. According to noted dog expert Stanley Coren, author of *How Dogs Think,* we would have been lost without them. "Without herding dogs," Coren contends, "the progress of civilization would have been much slower because we would not have had the organized animal husbandry that provides us with meat, wool, leather, and many other needed products."

Herding dogs—also known as working dogs—perform their tasks not so much through training but because of their natural instincts. Herding dogs have the same pack-hunting instincts as wolves. By studying how wolves hunt, scientists learned why and how dogs herd.

When a pack of wolves goes on a hunt, it tries to encircle a group of prey animals in order to keep those animals together. If seven wolves are in the pack, six will station themselves at roughly equidistant points along the circle. The wolves charge after the prey, nipping at their heels to keep them in line. Meanwhile, one wolf often waits in hiding, preparing to ambush a stray. The wolves' goal is to keep the prey animals together and isolate one stray, which they would kill.

When a herding dog herds sheep, he performs all the functions of the wolf pack. He starts at point A, stops, encircles up to point B, stops, and then continues along the circumference to point C, where he stops again. Determined to star in every part of this play, the herding dog also drops to the ground and stares at the sheep, playing the part of the wolf-in-ambush. The dog, of course, does not kill this sheep, but his fierce gaze scares the sheep into thinking that it better stay with the flock. The herding dog, playing the parts of several wolves, is thus able to keep the sheep or cattle or goats all bunched together.

When humans first discovered this ability in canines, they realized that they could use it to their advantage. With a few basic instructions, they could teach these dogs to herd on command—and move the flock in a particular direction.

A herding dog recognizes the shepherd (or farmer, handler, etc.) as an "alpha wolf," the leader of the herding process. Thus, after proper training, the dog will follow the shepherd's commands. When the shepherd says, "come-bye," the dog goes clockwise around the stock. "Away" means counterclockwise. "Cast" means to gather the stock in a group, and "look back" means to return for a missing animal. When the shepherd says "enough" or "that'll do," the dog stops working and returns to its master.

Lore Haug, a veterinarian at Texas A&M University, compares the handler-dog relationship to Fred Astaire and Ginger Rogers. "It really is like having a dance partner in a sense: the more they practice, the more subtle the communication becomes," Haug says. "A good herding dog can anticipate what the handler will tell them next."

There are more than eighty breeds of herding dogs, including various breeds of sheepdogs, collies, and shepherds. Even some smaller breeds, such as Welsh corgis, have herding ability. Different breeds have different skills. Dogs known as "heelers" nip at the animals' heels, while other breeds, such as border collies, use their strong stares to keep the animals in line. Border collies are often hailed as the preeminent herding animals. Mike Northwood, a farmer and dog trainer, calls them "class on grass."

Besides their herding instinct, these working dogs bring other powers to the job. They are speedy enough to encircle the flock, and they possess the stamina to work through the day.

States Coren, "When it comes to controlling a flock of sheep, a single shepherd and one dog do better than ten men without the assistance of a dog."

While a human worker would collapse from exhaustion or demand better working conditions, herding dogs work without complaint. According to Colleen Paige, an animal behaviorist, working dogs *need* to herd. Turning a herding dog into a domesticated city dog, she says, is "like taking someone who is naturally a fantastic painter and making him work a desk job—eventually, he'll go postal."

The domesticated herding dog, in the absence of sheep or cattle, will try to herd people. They will deliberately bump into them or perhaps nip at their heels. These dogs need to be trained to stop doing this.

One dog, Lucky, wasn't properly trained. A Bouvier des Flandres (a cattle-herding breed), Lucky belonged to Ronald Reagan when he was president of the United States. Out of instinct, Lucky often nipped at people's heels and rear ends—including the President's. Once, she bit into Reagan's pants and punctured his skin.

That was the last straw, as Lucky was shipped to the Reagan ranch in California. If it were a demotion, Lucky couldn't have cared less. No longer cooped up in Washington, she was able to run around and herd real animals—and not just presidents.

Chapter Thirty-Two

Guiding Lights

Power to Lead the Blind

Years ago in Florida, a blind woman and her guide dog walked up to a street and stopped. Though it was quiet—no cars to be heard—the dog refused to cross the road. The woman, certain they were safe, urged the pooch to lead the way, but he wouldn't budge.

When she finally got home, the woman told her husband about the episode. Had the dog disobeyed her for no good reason, or was there a logical explanation? The husband got in his car and drove back to that same location, where he found—lying in the middle of the street, as quiet as could be—an alligator.

The woman's dog had demonstrated "intelligent disobedience," the most important attribute of every guide dog. Dogs that are trained to lead the blind (and those of limited sight) follow their handlers' commands *except* when such commands would put the person in danger. Guide dogs save owners' lives because they are smart enough to disobey.

Blind people across the world are able to live independently due to the guide dogs' remarkable skills. Zerline Johnson is blind, but she gets around New York City thanks to Margo, a black Labrador retriever. "She takes me everywhere," Johnson says. "She's allowed everywhere the public is allowed: hospitals, grocery stores. She even goes to church every Sunday. I tell her to lay down and say her prayers."

The Seeing Eye, Inc., with headquarters in Morristown, New Jersey, and Toronto, is the oldest existing guide dog school in the world, dating back to 1929. That organization and others breed, raise, and train dogs to help the blind and visually impaired. Seeing Eye breeds German shepherds, Labrador retrievers, and golden retrievers—as well as boxers for those who are allergic to longhaired dogs.

Early on, the Seeing Eye dog lives an eventful life. At around eight weeks old, the puppy moves in with a volunteer trainer, who teaches it basic obedience. At eighteen months, the dog goes back to Seeing Eye, where it works for four months with an instructor. If the dog passes this phase, it is matched with a blind person. For four solid weeks, the blind person trains with the dog under the supervision of the instructor. After that, the dog moves in with its new owner.

While guide dogs are trained to help around the home—for example, picking up objects that fall on the floor—they are most helpful in public. The dog learns to walk at the handler's pace and on the person's left side. Because the owner usually knows the route, he or she will take the lead, with the dog obeying commands. "Forward," "left," or "right" the handler will say. Despite distractions, such as other dogs or tempting smells, the guide dog must stay on task. According to The Seeing Eye, pedestrians should not disturb the working guide dog.

When the dog reaches a curb or stairs, it will stop until the owner tells it how to proceed. The guide dog helps its human friend navigate buses and subways, and it avoids leading the person on a potentially troublesome path. Over time, the dog will learn the owner's complete route. "Go to the post office," the handler will say, and the dog will lead the way.

At an intersection, neither the blind person nor the dog can see the traffic lights. But with his or her strong sense of hearing, the handler can usually tell when there are no cars around. "Forward," the handler will say. The dog will proceed but only if it also believes that it is safe to cross. In modern times, intersections have become more difficult to navigate. Traffic is heavier, cars are quieter, and drivers are more in a rush. The biggest danger might be right-hand turners. Handlers may not be able to hear them, and dogs may not be aware of what's sneaking up on their rear-left.

Thanks to the Americans with Disabilities Act, guide dogs are guaranteed access to public places, including stores, libraries, doctors' offices, restaurants, etc. Despite this legal right, some establishments won't let the dogs through their doors. Such encounters are humiliating for the handlers and insulting to the dogs, who actually are trained to behave properly in such places.

Besides being mentally alert at all times, guide dogs need to be physically fit. Leading an elderly blind person down stairs requires exceptional strength—not to mention patience. By nature, dogs like to race up and down stairs. But a guide dog, according to Mark Derr, author of *Dog's Best Friend,* "has no luxury." Descending at an unnaturally slow pace, Derr maintains, the dog "must keep its weight well back on its haunches. You can see and feel its muscles straining, the pressure placed on its body, its concentration. A dog with bad hips will break down; one prone to impatience will crack under the pressure."

Due to the physical demands, the typical guide dog works only until age seven or eight. In the precious years that they're together, guide dogs and their owners develop extraordinary bonds. Such was the case with Omar Rivera and his dog, Dorado. A blind computer technician, Rivera worked on the seventy-first floor of New York City's World Trade Center's north tower before the building was destroyed in the infamous 9/11 attack. Dorado was asleep at his feet on the morning of September 11, 2001, when a hijacked airliner struck the tower—twenty-five stories above them.

In the midst of the smoke and screaming, Rivera felt he had no chance of escaping. But Dorado might make it, he thought, so he unleashed his dog and bid him adieu. Dorado, however, had other ideas. After leaving for a couple minutes, the dog returned to his owner and pushed him toward an emergency stairway. With additional help from Rivera's boss, the blind man and his dog descended the jammed-pack staircase. After an hour, they finally reached the street and ran to safety—just moments before the north tower collapsed.

"It was then that I knew for certain he loved me just as much as I loved him...," Rivera says. "I owe my life to Dorado—my companion and best friend."

—Chapter Thirty-Three—
Good Soldiers

Power to Serve
Its Country

On a hot spring day in Iraq in 2008, Staff Sergeant Joseph Evans demonstrated what his trained dog, Arzan, could do to a hostile insurgent. Evans slipped a thick protective sleeve on his arm and gave his Belgian Malinois the attack signal. A mighty animal, this breed of dog can run faster than 35mph and bite down with bone-crushing force. In attack mode, Arzan chomped hard on Evans' sleeve, sinking his teeth all the way to his skin and drawing blood. Without the protection, he could have chewed his arm to shreds. It gives an insurgent something to think about.

Not since the Vietnam War had the United States employed large numbers of dogs for military purposes. But during the Iraq War, these special canines have proved invaluable. More than one thousand "soldier dogs" have served nobly during the long, dangerous conflict. With their extraordinary powers, these dogs have performed operations that even the ablest Marines and Navy SEALS couldn't possibly accomplish. Dogs have been trained for the following duties: ·· Sniff out roadside bombs (which are responsible for most soldier casualties) ·· Sniff wires that are used to booby-trap buildings ·· Be on the "smell-out" for car bombs ·· Detect narcotics ·· Sniff out illegal weapons at checkpoints and border crossings ·· Track suspected insurgents ·· Attack on demand ·· Subdue detainees ·· Participate in crowd control

In a 2007 *Washington Post* article, federal official Terry Bohan recounted a few of the war dogs' recent accomplishments: In Iraq, a dog sniffed out a five hundred-pound bomb. In Egypt, a dog working with a SWAT team detected a booby trap on the house of a terrorist. And in Mexico, a dog uncovered a shipment of guns. Staff Sergeant Tony Davis, who served at Talil Air Force Base in central Iraq, says that his dog sniffed out a bomb strapped under an eighteen-wheel truck.

Moreover, the dogs' power to love has worked wonders, too. In March 2008, the *Houston Chronicle* reported that two black Labradors had been sent to Iraq to calm the nerves of overly stressed soldiers. As Staff Sergeant Chris Ebeling told *The* (Colorado Springs) *Gazette,* "No matter how bad a mood you are in, the dog is always happy to see you."

Canine "soldiers" first made their mark during World War II, when the U.S. War Dog Program enlisted more than ten thousand dogs for training. The "K9 Corps," as it was called, relied on five breeds: German shepherds, Doberman pinschers, Belgian sheepdogs, farm collies, and giant schnauzers. Ninety percent served as sentry dogs, which barked at suspected strangers. Quiet, intelligent dogs toiled as scouts, looking out for snipers and other enemies plotting to ambush. Messenger dogs carried messages from one of their handlers to another, and mine dogs sniffed for mines, trip wires, and booby traps.

Some WWII dogs went beyond the call of duty, including the fabled sentry dog Chips. In Sicily, Chips ran from his handler and attacked a machine gun crew in an enemy pillbox, seizing one of them and prompting the others to surrender.

During the Vietnam War, some 4,300 dogs served in the U.S. military, with 281 dying in the line of duty. In Iraq, the numbers have been much smaller, especially the fatalities. More than two hundred dogs per year have been trained for the Department of Defense at Lackland Air Force Base in Texas. In addition, the military has hired private contractors to train war-ready dogs.

Trainers have stuck with dogs of certain breeds. The German shepherd and Belgian Malinois make for powerful attack dogs, while Labrador retrievers have been employed for their extraordinary sense of smell. Even within these breeds, trainers look for dogs with certain dispositions. They prefer those who are playful—even hyper—with exceptional stamina. "We have dogs that are bouncing off the wall, wild-horse dogs," says Bohan. "We channel that energy into detection."

The *Washington Post* told the story of a rambunctious yellow Lab named Ricky Bobby, who was about to be put to sleep after being kicked out of three homes. The dog's life was saved at the eleventh hour, and he went on to serve as an antiterrorist dog in Morocco.

Trainers prefer to work with dogs that are twelve to eighteen months old. Using food rewards, the trainers can—over time—get the dogs to do seemingly anything. Dogs are triggered to respond to words and tones of voice—as well as whistles, clicks, and even hand signals. They are trained on leash and off leash. A dog might roam five hundred feet from its handler to sniff out a dangerous explosive.

During the Iraqi summers, soldiers have struggled to keep the dogs cool and healthy. A retailer called Helping Udders in Wichita, Kansas, has provided specialty clothing for "dogs in heat." They have supplied the military with cooling vests as well as "mutt luks," which protect the dogs' paws from the burning ground. Helping Udders has also supplied goggles for the dogs (called "doggles"), which shield their eyes from blowing desert sand.

These war dogs are loved and respected throughout the military. In fact, "Staff Sergeant Iron," a German shepherd, was "ranked" higher than his handler, Sergeant Joshua T. Rose. When Rose went on a mission, he carried with him a copy of an ode to police and military dogs. Part of the ode reads, "Trust in me, my friend, for I am your comrade. I will protect you with my last breath. When all others have left you and the loneliness of the night closes in, I will be at your side."

Tragically, these heavy words became all too real on July 6, 2007. Corporal Kory D. Wiens, age twenty, died along with his war dog, a white Lab named Cooper, when a bomb exploded in Muhammad Sath, Iraq. At the request of his family, Wiens and Cooper were buried together at Salt Creek Cemetery in Dallas, Oregon.

"Kory referred to Cooper as his son," says Master Sergeant Matt McHugh, "that's how much of a team they were."

PART IX
Melting Our Hearts
A Friend Indeed

—Chapter Thirty-Four—
Say "Cheese!"

Power to Elicit a Smile

They are the highlight of *America's Funniest Videos*—and the premium content of Animal Planet. They are...The Dogs That Make Us Chuckle. We smile, laugh, and shriek in excitement when we see a sheepdog jumping rope or a tiny pup running with a dumbbell in its mouth, its back legs off the ground. We howl in delight for the multitalented mutt that skateboards down the sidewalk, and what could be more uproarious than a schnauzer with its head stuck in a box of Lucky Charms? Or a black Lab chasing its tail in circles? Or the Dalmatian that can actually ride a bicycle?

With the possible exception of the Dramatic Prairie Dog and the Cats That Look Like Hitler, dogs make us smile more than any other creature. From Shih Tzus to Lhasa Apsos, dogs have us grinning from ear to ear with their boundless energy, frantic movements, furry faces, floppy ears, button noses, and ecstatic greetings when we get home from work. "Dogs are mood lifters because they are joyous creatures," exclaims Audrey Pavia. "It's hard to be depressed when a happy, bouncy dog is licking your face or acting goofy by running around the yard like a maniac with a toy in his mouth."

Humans have two kinds of smiles. One of them, which is under the control of the cerebral cortex, is conscious, voluntary. We employ this intentional smile when we politely thank our waitress. The other kind of smile, which involves the brain's basal ganglia, is spontaneous, involuntary. When we are suddenly happy, amused, or excited, our facial muscles contract, creating a beaming smile. Dogs, of course, amuse us with their charms and make us happy and excited when they burst into the room. That's why we always seem to be smiling whenever we greet them.

Mary Burch has her own theory about why dogs make us smile: "We all want to be loved, and only dogs provide us with the unconditional love that can make us smile on our worst days. Our dogs don't care if we are rich or poor, high-powered executives or unemployed—they are always happy to see us and they greet us as though the earth and stars revolve around our every move."

The exuberance of a loved one tends to make us smile, especially when he or she offers to share that exuberance with us. Imagine if your preschool-age daughter just finished writing a Valentine about you. She is proud and thrilled with her creation, and she runs excitedly across the room asking you to read it. Certainly this would make you smile. Now imagine if you walk in the door and your Labradoodle can't contain herself. She runs and gets her favorite toy, then brings it to you while wagging her tail. "We may be adults, but dogs invite us to play and enjoy life," Burch writes. "They model for us how to wake up full of joy every single morning and how to get the greatest pleasure out of something so simple, such as finding a ball to play with."

Often, the more we reciprocate the dog's playfulness—with smiles and laughter—the more excited and goofy-cute they become. As British humorist P. G. Wodehouse quips, "It is fatal to let any dog know that he is funny, for he immediately loses his head and starts hamming it up."

Burch remembers such a moment at a performance activity. "In a recent agility trial where dogs go over a six-foot A-frame, one dog ran to the top of the A-frame, looked out as though he was on a mountaintop, and barked continuously at the crowd," Burch recalls. "The crowd cheered and applauded for this spontaneous expression of excitement from the dog more than they did for the nationally ranked dogs who ran the course perfectly."

Oftentimes, a dog will prompt a warm, emotional smile. Veterinarian/author James Herriot inspired millions of such smiles with his many touching dog tales. In one story, Her-riot recalls a large-breed dog named Brandy, who as a puppy often sat on Mrs. Westby's lap as she weaned him. While doing so, she often wore a pair of blue jeans. After Brandy grew up, Mrs. Westby would not allow him to jump or climb on her lap because he was too big. But when she wore those old blue jeans, it sparked nostalgia in old Brandy. Desperately wanting to sit on his owner's blue-jeaned lap—but realizing that he wasn't allowed to jump or climb on her—Brandy tried a different tactic. He backed up to her blue jeans and slowly climbed up on her legs with his rear paws. Brandy would reach a point where he was almost doing a handstand. At such a sight, Mrs. Westby would always smile at Brandy's determination—and sweet intention.

Myra Savant, a registered nurse and expert on canine reproduction, normally takes a clinical approach to dogs. But while watching the morning routine of her personal pup, a Cavalier King Charles named Toby, she could only shake her head and grin. "Every day he would search through the house, the laundry, and all the bathrooms until he found a small towel—hand towels being his favorites," Savant recalls. "He would place his little towel carefully on the couch, using his paws to make sure it was flat. Then, he would begin his search for each of his toys...and as he found each one, he would jump up on the couch and place it on his towel. When he had a nice little stack of his personal belongings on his towel, he would sit next to his treasures and guard them from the other dogs. This little activity could keep him busy most of the morning."

For Toby, it was serious business. But even the serious dog makes us smile.

Chapter Thirty-Five

Regular Joes

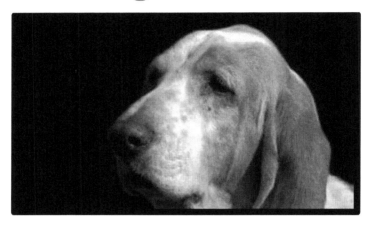

Power to Avoid the Pitfalls of Ego

With a new baby, two other children, and a troubled relationship with her man, Deanna didn't need any more drama in her life. When she visited an anti-cruelty society, and heard all the noisy barking, she wondered what the heck she was even doing there. But then she saw Angel, a large Labrador-Saint Bernard mix with kindly eyes. "I reached into the little hole of the pen and she came up and flipped my hand onto her head with her nose," Deanna recalls. "I laughed at this; she was strong, but yet so gentle. She wasn't jumping or barking, just sitting there happy to have my hand on her head."

Unlike the people in Deanna's life, Angel didn't come with "issues." She was a humble, gentle dog. With Angel, "I realized I was happier," Deanna recalls. "I still had moments of sadness of course but it was like Angel could sense them… she always came to me and put her head on my shoulder like she was giving me a hug…. On particularly sad days if I was on the couch or my bed, she'd get right up on my lap and curl up."

The story of Angel the humble dog helps us understand the meanings of *egoism* and *egotism*. The words are seemingly the same, but that *T* in the middle explains a profound difference between dogs and humans.

Egoism means that individuals are motivated by self-interest. This is true for both dogs and people. Dogs want food and their tummies rubbed, and people want to make money and enjoy the spoils. Conversely, both species exhibit altruistic behavior, meaning a concern for others.

But people—and not dogs—display egotism, which *Webster's Collegiate Dictionary* defines as "an exaggerated sense of self-importance." Egotistical, or vain, people want to enhance their self-importance and let everyone know how great they are.

It could be argued that egotism is just a manifestation of proving one's dominance—a natural instinct of many animal species. In a dominance hierarchy, individuals try to assert their dominance, since those at the top of the hierarchy obtain greater access to food, space, and sexual opportunities. This behavior is dramatically demonstrated among mountain goats, whose males batter each other with horns during mating season.

This behavior, however, is less evident in dogs. Scientists have struggled to prove that a dog dominance hierarchy exists because dogs have been domesticated for thousands of years. Scientists used to compare dogs to wolves, which seemed to have a hierarchy within each pack—headed by the most dominant of all, the alpha male. However, research in recent years has shown that even wolves don't seem to have a strict dominance hierarchy.

"[I]n natural wolf packs," contends Dr. L. David Mech, author of numerous books on wolves, "the alpha male or female are merely the breeding animals, the parents of the pack, and dominance contests with other wolves are rare, if they exist at all. During my thirteen summers observing the Ellesmere Island pack, I saw none."

If wolves don't demonstrate their dominance—that is, show the others how great they are—then it reasons that dogs don't display this behavior, either. Based on the views of pet behaviorist Dr. Peter Neville, the sole dog in the family home does not try to assert dominance. "There is strictly no such thing [as human-dog hierarchy]," he says. "People are predominantly parent figures to their dogs, not pack leaders in hierarchical arrangements, and there is a wealth of science from evolutionary biologists such as Professor Ray Coppinger to substantiate that view."

The family dog might bark, growl, or fuss to get what he wants (displaying egoism), but he apparently is not trying to prove that he's No. 1 or flaunt himself as Mr. Hot Stuff. In other words, dogs do not display egotism. Indeed, it's just the opposite; dogs are wonderfully humble creatures. In the words of Charles Darwin, "Man himself cannot express love and humility by external signs so plainly as does a dog, when with dropping ears, hanging lips, flexuous body, and wagging tail, he meets his beloved master."

Unfortunately, people—at least many of us—are not so humble. We see egotism expressed by the executive driving a BMW with a license plate that says "UNDR PAR." Bearded professors who pontificate, teenage girls with affected speech, Wall Street brokers with "power ties," and sexy people in risqué outfits display egotistical behavior. So do those who boast of their six-figure income, their child's .400 batting average, or the fact that "we don't eat sugar *or* watch television." Egotistical behavior often is detrimental to the individual, as others tend to dislike such vanity rather than be impressed by it.

Sometimes, egotism leads to tragic and even catastrophic outcomes. Fights and wars may not start because of egotistical tendencies, but they do often escalate because of them. Those who are attacked often respond with a "we'll show them who's boss" attitude, which leads to a greater counterattack. The conflict can thus turn into a "pissing contest" that escalates out of control. Fortunately, dogs don't desire to conquer the world—or even the household. Explains Lynn Hoover, a certified dog behavior consultant: "Dogs get themselves into predicaments, and we laugh at them and bail them out. Most are utterly unashamed, ready for their next adventure."

Egotists may want to pay less attention to themselves and more to dogs like Angel. They might learn a valuable lesson in humility.

Chapter Thirty-Six

Lean on Me

Power to Comfort in Times of Sorrow

Shaken by the tragedy at the Sandy Hook Elementary School, in which twenty first-grade students and six educators were shot to death, Tim Hetzner knew what he had to do. The Illinois father of four rounded up his eight golden retrievers—trained as "comfort dogs"—and his team of handlers, and they traveled to Newtown, Connecticut. Like he had done in the aftermath of Hurricane Sandy, Hetzner and his team sought to help those who were grieving.

During such horrific times, children are in need of comforting. They may not find it from grown-ups, who are upset themselves, but they can always find peace in a warm, calm, face-licking dog. So can adults.

Hetzner recalled his Newtown experience to the *Chicago Tribune.* "One lady came up to the dogs," he said. "She sat down, looking directly at them, and began to speak with the dogs, not the handlers." In tears, the woman spoke quietly to the animals. "Five people were killed on my block," she explained to them. "I have five funerals to go to. I don't know what to do. What can I possibly say to their families?"

Hetzner had seen such reactions before. "They're really just furry counselors," Hetzner explained. "They keep whatever they're told confidential, and they don't even take notes."

The Good Dog Foundation therapy teams also arrived at Newtown, as they would in Boston after the Boston Marathon bombing in 2013. In Newtown, Good Dog Foundation handler Lucian Lipinsky de Orlov brought Ronan, an Australian shepherd service dog, to a fifth-grade classroom. "There were so many students needing some 'dog time,'" Lipinsky told the *Lewisboro* (N.Y.) *Ledger*, "that I couldn't even see Ronan under all the petting and rubbing hands."

Lipinsky noted that for children, dogs are two things that adults may not be: anonymous and nonjudgmental. Just like stuttering readers can read more easily to dogs than to people, grieving children feel more at ease with friendly canines. "While in the class—at least for a while—the trauma of recent events went away," Lipinsky said.

The Good Dog Foundation oversees more than a thousand animal-assisted therapy teams. Each year, handlers and their four-legged healers visit more than three hundred facilities and

300,000 people in need, from families of victims at disaster sites to wounded veterans to hospitalized children.

Just as nobly, the Lutheran Church Charities K-9 Comfort Dogs also reach out their paws. After the Boston Marathon bombing, representatives of the program went to work. Dogs Luther, Ruthie, and Isiah arrived at the First Lutheran Church of Boston to console those in need. They also visited local hospitals to comfort survivors of the blast, which had killed three people and injured more than 260 others.

The dogs were also dispatched to Boston-area hospitals to comfort survivors who could not visit them at the church. "Animals have an uncanny ability to discern that you and I have sadness and distress," Reverend Ingo Dutzmann, a pastor at the church, told *The Huffington Post.* "Rather than shying away from it, they're attracted to it."

Comfort dogs have helped people during many recent tragedies. In March 2014, a massive mudslide in Oso, Washington, killed more than forty people. After the horrific event, the Green Cross Academy of Traumatology called for Animal Assisted Crisis Response volunteers. More than a dozen teams spent time in the Oso area, including dogs Monroe and Pongo, who comforted survivors and helped emergency responders relieve some stress.

At the Washington Navy Yard in 2013, a shooter took the lives of thirteen people. The U.S. Navy called on the services of HOPE Animal Assisted Crises Response, which brought in thirty-four dog teams from ten states to provide support for those in need.

After a 2011 tornado devastated Joplin, Missouri, killing 158 people in the area, dogs Louie and Jackson arrived to help. "We put them to work soon after the tornado," Jason Glaskey, minister of youth and families at Immanuel Lutheran Church in Joplin, told *The Joplin Globe*. "They provide comfort and a way for people to get their feelings out.... They serve as a bridge for conversation. As people pet the dogs, they are able to open up and talk about what is affecting them."

After Louie and Jackson spent a year and a half in Joplin, the two dogs were prepped for a more urgent mission: Newtown. They climbed into a van and drove more than 1,300 miles to the devastated city.

"When people started collecting at the [Newtown] vigils," Glaskey told the *Globe*, "the dogs helped them go through the mourning process. After that, we were invited to be a part of the counseling effort, and we have been there ever since."

It turns out that comfort dogs can heal more than the victims; they can also do wonders for their handlers. In Illinois, a Harper College course teaches students to handle dogs deployed to natural disasters and other tragic events. The spring 2014 course was so popular that there was a waiting list to get in. Merv Daehler, a seventy-one-year-old retired veterinarian, was one of the lucky twenty students who gained admittance.

Daehler, who had suffered a stroke four years earlier, wasn't expected to survive. He had to learn to walk again, and he had trouble holding onto a dog's leash. Still, he was determined to graduate the class and become a valuable member of the K-9 Comfort Dogs Ministry. He still felt that "there was some purpose" left in his life, and "maybe this is part of it."

Chapter Thirty-Seven

Man's Best Friend

Power to Exhibit Unmatched Loyalty

To football fans, the name "Heidi" conjures memories of the best finish no one saw—a 1968 NFL thriller between the Raiders and Jets that NBC abandoned in the final minutes to show the movie *Heidi* at its regularly scheduled time.

To animal behaviorists, the name "Heidi" elicits a much more moving story. Heidi, a Jack Russell terrier, earned acclaim as Scotland's most loyal dog in 2001, when her owner fell some five hundred feet to his death while hiking in the hills of Altnaharra. For two days, no one knew the whereabouts of sixty-five-year-old Graham Snell.

When rescue teams found him, at an elevation of about 1,200 feet, Heidi was standing guard over the body, having coaxed her way down the rugged terrain some forty-eight hours prior to watch faithfully over her master.

That show of canine loyalty is hardly an isolated one.

North of Denver in 2008, rancher Kip Konig saw a German shepherd running toward him, then running back toward a partially obscured pickup truck in the Pawnee National Grasslands. Konig got the feeling the dog was trying to show him something—or someone—so he went to investigate. What Konig found was shocking and sad.

Near the truck were the skeletal remains of the dog's owner, a twenty-five-year-old man who is thought to have shot himself six weeks earlier. The dog, Cash, had been guarding his master's body the entire time, surviving by hunting mice and rabbits.

"She was Jake's baby," says the wife of the suicide victim after being reunited with the dog. "She was our baby before we had our son. They would play fetch for ever and ever."

Those are recent stories, but dogs have been recognized for their powerful loyalty dating back to ancient times. Chinese folklore attaches characteristics to people born in certain years, and those born in the Year of the Dog are said to have a "deep sense of loyalty."

What accounts for the uncanny loyalty of dogs? Well, certainly there is a behavioral component at work. Living beings become attached to those who give them sustenance. As the old adage goes, you don't bite the hand that feeds you. However, experts point out that the loyalty of dogs goes well beyond what science would expect in a behavioral bond between animal and human.

"If you want someone who will love you forever," insists Mary Burch, "get a dog. Dogs have been bred for centuries to be loyal to their humans. While there is no doubt a behavioral component to loyalty, canine loyalty goes far beyond a behavioral response. For owners who have raised their dogs right, particularly when dogs come into a home as puppies, bonding takes place that will last a lifetime."

Burch points to a story that—like the tale of Cash—shows that sometimes such bonding lasts even longer than a lifetime, and can bring nations to immortalize their four-legged heroes with statues.

A small bronze statue sits in Tokyo's Shibuya Train Station honoring Hachiko, Japan's most faithful dog. The Akita, beginning in 1924, accompanied his owner, Eisaburo Uyeno, to the station each day when he left for work. When Uyeno returned, the dog would be waiting, his tail wagging. It was the daily routine until one day in 1925, when Uyeno became ill on the job and died before he could return home.

Hachiko, just two years old at the time, continued to wait. And wait. And wait. The dog would stand at the station waiting for his master to come home, sometimes staying there for weeks at a time. Commuters witnessed the touching vigil again and again for a full decade before "Hachi" finally was reunited with his long-lost friend in death in 1935.

"Loyalty like this," Burch notes, "makes it easy to see why dogs are man's and woman's best friend."

Animal behaviorists point out that dogs are

pack animals, having descended from wolves, and that their evolution contributes to their loyalty. As masters in charge of feeding and care, humans generally are seen as "pack leaders" by domestic dogs. Hence, the dogs follow. And they follow faithfully.

Most breeds of dogs have also "devolved" to the point where their "hunting skills" are all but gone. This, of course, is a good thing for those who prefer to be licked and nuzzled at the end of the work or school day, rather than walking through the door to the risk of a more dangerous confrontation with a four-legged creature.

More independent animals, such as cats, might prefer to keep their distance, though many are certainly "cuddlers." However, dog owners will tell you there's nothing quite like the greeting a pooch provides—even after just a few minutes away from its master.

"If dogs get what they need—food, shelter, a soft bed, a pack to call their own, lots of lovin' and playtime—they are happy," asserts Lynn Hoover, a certified dog behavior consultant. "Humans are not so easily contented. They have the 'better than you' syndrome. That is, they'll be your friend as long as they can feel 'better than' you.

"Dogs say, 'yeah, yeah, we both know you're better. Now throw the ball, gimme a treat, walk with me, and if you're leaving, come home soon.'"

End of Story.
Hope you enjoyed our book! *Les & Dave*

ABOUT THE AUTHORS

Les Krantz with Tillie. Les is a former veterinary technician in the U.S Air Force where he received his veterinary training. Since then, he has authored more than 50 books on a variety of subjects. When not writing books, he heads the book publishing company Facts That Matter, Inc.

David Aretha, with Wingnut, is an award-winning author of dozens of books and coauthor of the original *Power of the Dog* and editor of the *Practical Guide to Dog Care* and more than 100 nonfiction books. He wrote a screenplay and comic strip based on his cockapoo, *Waffle*.

—— Throw us a bone! ——

Write a review of our book.
on your favorite online retail website

Acknowledgements

To be engaged in the creation of this book was a joy in every way, even though it was painstakingly researched. It was written using the latest and best research on canine behavior. There were many involved, and the coauthors would like to convey our appreciation to all, especially to the contributing writers.

A special thank you goes to Caroline Coile, Ph.D., who vetted the manuscript. She is the author of 30 books and hundreds of articles on dogs, including the highly acclaimed book *Barron's Encyclopedia of Dog Breeds*. Dr. Coile is a former researcher in canine sensory systems and has published in the fields of canine vision and audition. She also has worked as a consultant to the FAA on dog olfaction.

Many veterinarians, trainers, and canine behaviorists also contributed their time. They include: Nan Arthur, owner of Whole Dog Training in El Cajon, California; Janice Biniok, active in therapy dog work and author of several books about companion animals; Mary Burch, certified applied animal behaviorist and author of several dog books; Cynthia Cook of Veterinary Vision, Inc. in San Francisco, a veterinarian and opthamologist; Marc Goldberg, a certified dog trainer and president of the International Association of Canine Professionals; James E. Hagedorn, veterinarian in Evanston, Illinois; Kaylan Head, founder of Full Circle Obedience School in Oklahoma City; Lynn Hoover, an animal behavior specialist and owner of Dog Quirks, LLC, in Pittsburgh; Audrey Pavia, former managing editor of *Dog Fancy* magazine and author of the award-winning book *The Labrador Retriever Handbook;* Gene Pavlovsky, veterinarian at the Animal Medical Center in Skokie, Illinois; Ed Presnall, dog trainer, tracking judge, and award-winning author; Myra Savant, registered nurse and expert on dog reproduction; Sara Scott, a certified pet trainer and behavioral counselor; Terry Seraceno, chairperson of the board of Dr. Paws Pet Assisted Therapy Dogs in Farmington Hills, Michigan; Jack L. Stephens, veterinarian, author, and founder of Pets Best Insurance; Chris Walkowicz, AKC judge and award-winning author; and Kari Winters, award-winning writer who has served as a psychiatric nurse and animal rescue worker.

Les Krantz, David Aretha

Bibliography

NOTE TO RESEARCHERS: In the list below, the automatic hyphens have been suppressed; therefore any hyphens shown in URLS below are part of the web address and are needed to find the information on the Internet.

Aarons, Maureen. *The Handbook of Autism: A Guide for Parents and Professionals*. New York: Routledge, 1991.

"About Guide Dogs." Assistance Dogs International, Inc., www. assistancedogsinternational.org/guide.php.

"All About Seizure Dogs." *Epilepsy Foundation*, December 1, 2001, www.epilepsyfoundation.org/epilepsyusa/aboutseizuredogs.cfm.

Allan, Ssuna Ambrose. "We can die but still live." *British Council InterAction*, May 24, 2007, www.bc-interaction.org/past_events/cultural_heritage/articles/we_can_die_but_still_live.

"Alpha Status, Dominance, and Division of Labor in Wolf Packs."

"Are greyhounds the fastest dog?" *Greyhound Zoom*, June 2008, www.greyhoundzoom.com/are-greyhounds-the-fastest-dog/.

Associated Press. "Jake, 9/11 rescue dog, takes his final stroll." *Newsday*, July 27, 2007.

Associated Press. "Papelbon says his dog chewed World Series ball." *USA Today*, December 20, 2007, www.usatoday.com/sports/baseball/al/redsox/2007-12-20-papelbon-ball-dog_N.htm.

Associated Press. "Rent-A-Dog at Swiss Resort Is Learning Japanese." *International News*, May 13, 1991.

Associated Press. "South Korea to use cloned dogs to sniff for drugs and explosives." *International Herald Tribune*, April 24, 2008, www.iht.com/articles/ap/2008/04/24/news/SKorea-Cloned-Dogs.php.

Associated Press. "Therapeutic dogs good for heart

patients." *MSNBC*, November 15, 2005,
http://www.msnbc.msn.com/id/10051979/.

"*Autism Spectrum Disorders Overview*." Centers for Disease Control and Prevention,
www.cdc.gov/ncbddd/autism/overview.htm.

"*Basic instinct: Animals sense danger*." The Times of India, January 9, 2005,
timesofindia.indiatimes.com/articleshow/984845.cms.

Battersby, Amy. "*Why Dogs, Like Humans, Love a Good Yawn*." Daily Express,
www.express.co.uk/posts/view/55610/Why-dogs-likeh umans-love-a-good-yawn-.

Bensinger, Greg. "*Dogs behaving badly? Give them a taste of sheep herding*." Columbia News Service, March 1, 2005, jscms.jrn.columbia.
edu/cns/2005-03-01/bensinger-herding.

Blumenfeld, Laura. "*They Sniff at Danger*." The Washington Post, August 30, 2007.

"*Border collie just loves to chew up those chair legs*." The Miami Herald, April 6, 2008,
www.miamiherald.com/357/story/482910.html.

Bradley, Richard. "*Jim the Wonder Dog*." A Rock in My Shoe, www. arockinmyshoe.com/wonderdog.html.

Brinkley, Lori. "*The Sport of Canine Weight Pulling FAQ*." Tri-State Alaskan Malamute Club,
www.tsamc.org/tsamc/faq/FAQ.html.

"*Bulldogs*." All Experts, May 29, 2007,
en.allexperts.com/q/
Bulldogs-2360/Bulldogs-Swimming.htm.

"*Can Dogs Sense Our Emotions?*" Pet Place,
www.petplace.com/
dogs/can-dogs-sense-our-emotions/page1.aspx.

"*Canada guide dog in language row*." BBC News, July 8, 2004, news.
bbc.co.uk/2/hi/americas/3874819.stm.

"*Canine Chewing*." Nebraska Humane Society,
www.
nehumanesociety.org/site/DocServer/caninechewing.
pdf?docID=186.

"*Canine ESP: Can Dogs Sense Danger?*" Small Dogs Paradise, January 12, 2008,
www.smalldogsparadise.com/case-studies/canine-esp

can-dogs-sense-danger/.

"Canine Feet." Dog Owner's Guide, www.canismajor.com/dog/feet.html.

Canon, Scott. "Pooch Keeps Pride Alive in Missouri." The Boston Globe, May 10, 1999.

Caras, Roger A. A Dog Is Listening. New York: Simon & Schuster, 2004.

Case, Linda P. The Dog: Its Behavior, Nutrition, and Health. Blackwell, 2005.

Cohen, J. A. and H. W. Fox. "Vocalization in Wild Canids and Possible Effects of Domestication." Behavioral Processes, 1, 1976.

Coile, Caroline. "Bringing Dog Vision into Focus." Working Dogs, www.workingdogs.com/vision_coile.htm.

Cook, Cynthia. "How Well Does Fido See? Cataract & Refractive Surgery Today, July 2008, www.crstoday.com/PDF%20Articles/0708/ CRST0708_05.pdf.

Coppinger, Lorna and Raymond Coppinger. Dogs: A Startling New Understanding of Canine Origin, Behavior, & Evolution. New York: Scribner, 2001.

Coren, Stanley. How Dogs Think. New York: Summit, 1992. The Intelligence of Dogs. New York: The Free Press, 1994. Why Does My Dog Act That Way? New York: Simon and Schuster, 2006.

Correa, Julio E. "The Dog's Sense of Smell." Alabama Cooperative Extension System, July 2005, www.aces.edu/pubs/docs/U/UNP-0066/ UNP-0066.pdf.

Dearth, Kim D. R. The Compassion of Dogs: Heartwarming Stories of Loyalty and Kindness. New York: Prima Publishing: 2002.

"Death and a Dog's Devotion Part I." Dogs in the News, July 4, 2001, dogsinthenews.com/issues/0107/articles/010704a.htm.

The Denver Post and Associated Press. "Dog guarded its owner for weeks after suicide." The Seattle Times, August 13, 2008, seattletimes. nwsource.com/html/nationworld/2008109752_loyaldog 13.html.

Derr, Mark. Dog's Best Friend: Annals of the Dog-Human Relationship. New York: Henry Holt, 1997.

Dodman, Nicholas H. *If Only They Could Speak: Stories About Pets and their People.* New York: W. W. Norton, 2002.

"Does Your Dog Paddle." *AZ Central,* July 15, 2008, www.azcentral.com/pets/articles/2008/07/15/20080 715dogswim.html.

"Dog bites and bite force," *Lassie, Get Help,* January 24, 2008, lassiegethelp.blogspot.com/2008/01/dog-bites-and-bit e-force.html.

"Dog gives up life to save man from fire." *Boston.com,* November 15, 2007, www.boston.com/news/odd/articles/2007/11/15/dog _gives_up_life_to_save_man_from_fire/?rss_id=Bos ton.com+--+News+of+the+odd.

"Dog Rescued After Four Months Stranded in Desert." *Gimundo,* March 14, 2008, www.gimundo.com/Articles/Daily/891.

"Dog Sense of Hearing." *See Fido,* www.seefido.com/html/dog sense_of_hearing.htm.

"The Dog Who Can Sense Death." *For the Love of the Dog,* 2007, petloverstips.com/ForTheLoveoftheDog/news-updates /the-dog-who-cansense-death.

"A Dog's Sudden Burst Of Speed." *For Your Canine,* December 11, 2007, foryourcanine.com/12/11/a-dogs-sudden-burst-of-spee d.

"The dogs of the Inuit: companions in survival." *Food and Agriculture Association of the United Nations,* www.fao.org/docrep/ w0613t/w0613t0m.htm.

"Dogs may be a diabetic's best friend." *Chicago Tribune,* February 10, 2008.

"Dogs Swallow the Darndest Things." *News Channel 5,* February 3, 2007, www.newschannel5.com/Global/story.asp?S=608323 1.

"Dogs And Thunderstorms." *Animal Wellness,* 2007, animalwellnesspei.com/?p=21.

"Dogs work 'magic' on kid with autism." *CNN,* July 18, 2008, www.cnn.com/2008/LIVING/07/16/heroes.shirk/.

Dolan, Kate, et al. "Epilepsy: A matter of coping." The Indianapolis Star, December 2, 2007.

Doyle, Alicia. "Service dogs can detect diabetics in danger." Ventura County Star, June 8, 2008.

"Driven to Discover Q&A." University of Minnesota College of Veterinary Medicine, www.cvm.umn.edu/newsandevents/facts/petsafety/Driven_to_Discover_Q26A.html.

Eden, R. S. "Dog Training For Law Enforcement." Eden Consulting Group, www.policek9.com/html/raisepup.html.

"Empowering Kids Who Have Autism." CBS News, April 16, 2008, www.cbsnews.com/stories/2008/04/16/earlyshow/health/main4019559. shtml.

"Endurance." Natural History Museum of Los Angeles County, www. nhm.org/exhibitions/dogs/formfunction/endurance.html.

"Evidence against dominance hierarchies and alpha theory." Dogster, www.dogster.com/forums/Behavior_and_Training/thread/553729.

Falkenburry, Cheryl. "Helping The Chew-A-Holic Dog." The Nature in Us, February 9, 2007, www.thenatureinus.com/2007/02/helping-chewholic-dog.html.

Farrar, Lara. "Electronic nose could spark end of sniffer dogs." CNN, August 1, 2008, www.cnn.com/2008/TECH/science/08/01/electro.nose/.

"Favorite Dog Quotes." Max's Corner, http://home.comcast.net/ ~maxcpoo/quotes.html.

"Five Basic Commands in Many Languages." Talking Tails, www. talkingtails.com/command.html.

"Five Dogs Incredible Stories of Loyalty and Valor." Pets Do, www. petsdo.com/blog/five-dogs-incredible-stories-loyalty-and-valor.

Fought, Tim. "Mountaineering experts: Fido should probably stay home." KGW, February 20, 2007, www.kgw.com/news-local/stories/

kgw_022007_news_mt_hood_climbers_dog.1c82852
9.html.

Fullwood, Janet. "To the rescue." The Sacramento
Bee, February 7, 2008.

"Gastric Foreign Body in a Dog." The Pet Center,
www.thepetcenter. com/xra/ball.html.

Gazit, Irit. "Domination of Olfaction Over Vision in
Explosives Detection by Dogs." Applied Animal
Behavior Science, www.bio-sense. com/files/do.pdf.

Gleason, Brian. "Family seeks dog detector for
diabetic seizures." Charlotte Sun, December 18, 2007.

Goldston, Linda. "Canine Lifeline." San Jose Mercury
News, November 22, 2007.

Gordon, Lee. "Animals' Sixth Sense Predicts Bad
Weather." Zootoo, July 25, 2008,
www.zootoo.com/petnews/animalssixthsensepredictsb
adwe.

Gorman, James. "Smell in Stereo? Most of Us Would
Just Say No." The New York Times, February 7, 2006.

Greenlee, Ted. "Temperature Adaptation in Northern
Dogs." Austin Web Publishing, Inc.,
www.awpi.com/Combs/Huskies/Cooling.html.

"The Growing Need for Animal-Assisted Therapy
and Activity." UCLA Health System,
www.uclahealth.org/body.cfm?id=67.

Grutz, Jane Waldron. "A King and Two Salukis."
Saudi Aramco World,
www.saudiaramcoworld.com/issue/200803/a.king.a
nd.two. salukis.htm.

"Guardians of the Night." Mid-Atlantic German
Shepherd Rescue,
www.magsr.org/ourheros.htm.

Hardcastle, Martha. "Gear helps military dogs stay
on guard for troops in Iraq." Dayton Daily News, April
3, 2008.

Harris, Tom. "How a Guide Dog Works." How Stuff
Works, animals.
howstuffworks.com/animal-facts/guide-dog.htm.

Hatherly, Joanne. "Wolf's fast track to doghood." The
Gazette (Montreal), April 2, 2007.

Herriot, James. James Herriot's Favorite Dog
Stories. New York: St. Martin's, 1986.

"History of the 1925 Nome Serum Run." *Balto's True Story*, www. baltostruestory.com/index.htm.

Horwitz, Debra F. "Canine Communication." *VIN*, www.vin.com/ VINDBPub/SearchPB/Proceedings/PR05000/PR00469. htm.

"How Safe is That Doggie in the Water?" *Boat U.S.*, November 2000, www.boatus.com/foundation/Findings/findingsdog.htm.

"How to Train a Rescue Dog." *See Fido*, www.seefido.com/html/ how_to_train_a_rescue_dog.htm.

"How Well Do Dogs See At Night?" *ScienceDaily*, November 9, 2007, www.sciencedaily.com/releases/2007/11/071108140336. htm.

Hungerford, Laura. "Dog Hearing." *Newton BBS*, www.newton.dep. anl.gov/askasci/vet00/vet00003.htm.

Ismail, Raviya H. "Canine warriors fight beside Marines." *The Miami Herald*, May 25, 2008.

Israelsen-Hartley, Sara. "Tiny dog uses big ruff-ruffs to take a bite out of crime." *The Deseret News*, February 26, 2008.

"It's Time to Paws and Reflect." *DogGone Charming*, www. doggonecharming.com/page/118544202.

"JimtheWonderDog." *JimtheWonderDog*, www.jimthew onderdog.com/.

Kelly, Jo. "The Canadian Eskimo Dog." *Sled Dog Central*, www. sleddogcentral.com/canadian_eskimo.htm.

Kilgore Bauer, Nona. *Dog Heroes of September 11th*. Freehold, N.J.: Kennel Club Books, 2006.

Kliers, Yael. "The Sweet Smell of Genetics." *The Jerusalem Report*, October 6, 2003.

Korman, Henry and Mary Ellen Korman. *Living with Dogs: Tales of Love, Commitment, and Enduring Friendship*. Tulsa, Okla.: Council Oak Books, 1997.

Lai, Eric. "The Sense of Smell." *South China Morning Post*, December 28, 2007.

Lemmon, Kathryn. "Greyfriars Bobby: The Loyal Skye Terrier." *Associated Content*, March 26, 2007, www.associatedcontent.com/

article/183333/greyfriars_bobby_the_loyal_skye_ter
rier.html.

Leong, Kristie. "Can a Pet Help Fight Depression?"
Gomestic, October 24, 2007,
www.gomestic.com/Pets/Can-a-Pet-Help-Fight-Depre
ssion.53907.

Levine, Samuel. "Dogs may help lower children's
blood pressure." Israel 21c, April 13, 2008,
http://www.israel21c.org/bin/en.jsp?enDispWho=Arti
cles%5El2067&enPage=BlankPage&enDisplay=view&
enDispWh at=object&enVersion=0&enZone=Health.

Lidz, Franz. "Pat C Rendezvous." Sports Illustrated,
June 13, 1994.

London, Rick. "Can A Dog Help Heal Major
Depression?" Ezine Articles,
ezinearticles.com/?Can-A-Dog-Help-Heal-Major-Depr
ession?&id=996424.

"Loyalty to fore in Year of the Dog. CNN, January
26, 2006, edition.cnn.
com/2006/WORLD/asiapcf/01/24/chinese.newyear/i
ndex.html.

Lundborg, Pam. "Guide-Dog Trainer Gets a State
Fair Treat." The Post-Standard, August 29, 2008.

"Make your next family pet a Retired Racing
Greyhound!" Greyhound Friends of North Carolina,
www.greyhoundfriends.com/
info%20on%20greys.htm.

Margolis, Anne. "How Canine Feet (Usually) Beat
the Cold." Wolf Song of Alaska,
www.wolfsongalaska.org/wolf_feet.htm.

Marks, Amber. "Smells Suspicious." The Guardian,
March 31, 2008,
http://www.guardian.co.uk/science/2008/mar/31/int
ernationalcrime.

Mayer, Karen Ott. "Grace and Garbo." The
Commercial Appeal, November 26, 2007.

McAllister, Rallie. "New ways to control seizures."
The Buffalo News, June 6, 2006.

McCord, Keith. "Dog found after surviving alone in
winter wilderness." KSL, March 14, 2008,
www.ksl.com/ ?nid=148&sid=2857200.

McKeon Charkalis, Diana. "Dogged Devotion." Daily

News of Los Angeles, December 26, 2005.

Miklosi, Adam. Dog Behaviour, Evolution, and Cognition. London: Oxford University Press, 2008.

"The Most Beautiful Real Life Dog Story Collection." Amazing Dog Stories, www.amazingdogstories.com/.

Mott, Maryann. "Did Animals Sense Tsunami Was Coming?" National Geographic News, January 4, 2005, news.nationalgeographic.com/news/2005/01/0104_050104_tsunami_animals_2.html.

Myrna, Milani. DogSmart. Lincolnwood, Ill.: Contemporary Books, 1997.

Nash, Bruce and Allan Zullo. Amazing But True Dog Tales. Kansas City: Andrews and McMeel, 1994.

"Nursing home's cat can sense death." Daily Times, July 27, 2007, www.dailytimes.com.pk/default.asp?page=2007%5C07%5C27%5Cstory_27-7-2007_pg9_8.

"Objects Consumed By Foolish Pets Cause Problems." University of Illinois at Urbana-Champaign College of Veterinary Medicine, September 17, 2001, vetmed.illinois.edu/petcolumns/showarticle.cfm?id=310.

O'Harra, Doug. "Built for speed and endurance." Anchorage Daily News, February 23, 1997, www.adn.com/adn/iditarod/25/perfect.html.

Offutt, Jason. "Jim the Wonder Dog." From the Shadows, March 13, 2007, from-the-shadows.blogspot.com/2007/03/jim-wonder-dog.html.

"OSU Veterinarian to Study Iditarod Dogs for Endurance Clues." Oregon State University, March 5, 2007, oregonstate.edu/dept/ncs/newsarch/2007/Mar07/iditarod.html.

"Our Story." Heaven Sent Paws, http://www.heavenscentpaws.com/ site/ourStory.htm.

O'Farrell, Peggy. "An epilepsy patient's best friend." The Cincinnati Enquirer, September 24, 2004.

"Pack Mentality in Dogs." Florida Pet Pages, www.floridapetpages.com/articles/PackMentalityInDogs.html.

Parente, Audrey. "These dogs of war put bite into fight." Daytona Beach News-Journal, March 13, 2008.

Perkins, Sid. "Electronic Noses Provide a New Sense of the Future." Science News, Vol. 157, No. 8, 2000.

"Pet dog sniffs out hidden drugs." BBC News, December 24, 2007, news.bbc.co.uk/1/hi/wales/southeast/7159300.stm.

"A Pilgrimage to Honor Hachiko, Japan's Most Faithful Dog." Fabulous Travel, www.fabuloustravel.com/index.php?option=com_resour ce&controller=article&article=21728&category_id=39 8.

Plonsky, Mark. "Canine Vision." University of Wisconsin-Stevens Point Psychology Department, October 17, 1998, www.uwsp.edu/ PSYCH/dog/LA/DrP4.htm.

Pothier, Dick. "Animals Help You Beat Stress." Philadelphia Inquirer, July 19, 1981.

PoweAllred,Alexandra. Dogs Most Wanted. Washington: Brassey's, 2004.

Prigg, Mark. "Scientists Scent Victory in Quest for Super Nose." The Sunday Times (London), January 11, 1998.

Raguso, Emilie. "Working Like a Dog." The Modesto Bee, September 3, 2007.

Reuters. "Mutt Saves Climbers at 21,000 Feet." Chicago Tribune, February 18, 1995.

Rice, Michael. Swifter than the Arrow: The Golden Hunting Hounds of Ancient Egypt. London: I. B. Tauris, 2006.

Ring, Elizabeth. Detector Dogs: Hot on the Scent. Millbrook Press: 1993.

Roeder, Tom. "Dogged Determination." The Gazette (Colorado Springs, Colo.), December 26, 2005.

Ropeik, David. "How and Why." The Boston Globe, December 6, 1999.

Ross, John. Dog Talk: Training Your Dog Through a Canine Point of View. New York: Macmillan, 1995.

Rozell, Ned. "A Man, His Dog and Two Earthquakes." Alaska Science Forum, February 13, 2003, http://www.gi.alaska.edu/ ScienceForum/ASF16/1633.html.

Russell, Michael. "Verbal Communication In Training The Dog." Ezine Articles, ezinearticles.com/?Verbal-Communication-In-Training-The-Dog&id=289966.

"Search and Rescue Dogs." Dog Owner's Guide, www.canismajor. com/dog/srchresc.html.

Scholting, Ronda. "Mountain Climbing Dog Saves Hikers'

Lives." *Zootoo*, August 7, 2008, www.zootoo.com/petnews/ highaltitudemountainclimbingdo.

Shewmake, Tiffin. *Canine Courage: The Heroism of Dogs.* Otsego, Mich.: PageFree Publishing, Inc., 2002.

"Sled Dog Racing." *42 Explore,* www.42explore2.com/sleddog.htm.

"Sled Dogs: An Alaskan Epic." *PBS,* www.pbs.org/wnet/nature/ sleddogs/balto.html.

Sohn, Emily. "A Sense of Danger." *Science News for Kids,* April 13, 2005, www.sciencenewsforkids.org/articles/20050413/Feature1.asp.

"Sopranos: resonance tuning and vowel changes." *The University of New South Wales,* www.phys.unsw.edu.au/jw/soprane.html.

"Speed of Animals." *Newton BBS,* January 30, 1982, www.newton. dep.anl.gov/natbltn/200-299/nb215.htm.

"Sprinter." *Time,* May 17, 1926, www.time.com/time/magazine/ article/0,9171,769359,00.html.

Squire, Ann. *Understanding Man's Best Friend: Why Dogs Look and Act the Way They Do.* New York: Macmillan, 1991.

Stall, Sam. "Dogs who made a difference." *Saturday Evening Post,* May-June 2008, http://findarticles.com/p/articles/mi_m1189/is_/ai_ n25436849.

"Stanley Coren on Dog Intelligence." *Smartdogs Weblog,* March 9, 2008, smartdogs.wordpress.com/2008/03/09/stanley-coren-on-dogi ntelligence/.

Stefko, Jill. "Dogs' Death Premonitions and Grief." *Suite 101,* May 17, 2007, paranormal.suite101.com/article.cfm/dogs_death_ premonitions_and_grief.

"The Psychic World of Dogs Part I." *Suite 101,* October 12, 2005, www.suite101.com/article.cfm/paranormal_ realm/118633.

Stephens, Jack. "Help Overcome Depression with a Dog." *Pets Best,* September 12, 2007, www.petsbest.com/Community/Blog/Help-Overcome-Depressi on-with-a-Dog.aspx.

"The Story." *Greyfriars Bobby,* www.greyfriarsbobby.co.uk/story.html.

"The Strange Things That Dogs Eat." *Itchmo,* August 14, 2007, www. itchmo.com/the-strange-things-that-dogs-eat-2210.

"Study: Pets curb dangerous rises in blood pressure." *CNN,* November 8, 1999, www.cnn.com/HEALTH/heart/9911/07/pets.heart.

Syrotuk, Bill. "Theory of Scent." *Eden Consulting Group*, *www. policek9.com/html/theory.html*.

Tan, Michelle. "Killed in Iraq, dog team buried together." *Army Times*, July 24, 2007, *www.armytimes.com/news/2007/07/army_canineteam_070722w/*.

Taylor, R.J.F. "The Work Output of Sledge Dogs." *Department of Zoology, University of Cambridge*, January 30, 1957, *www. pubmedcentral.nih.gov/picrender.fcgi?artid=1362974&bloblype=pdf*.

"The Three 'E's': Exercise, Endorphins and Euphoria." *Men's Total Fitness*, *www.mens-total-fitness.com/endorphins.html*.

"Top Dogs for Cold Climates." *Pet Place*, *www.petplace.com/dogs/top-dogs-for-cold-climates/page1.aspx*.

"Top 10 Things Dogs Shouldn't Eat, but Do." *Tummy Scratch*, January 24, 2008, *petsupplies4less.wordpress.com/2008/01/24/top-10things-dogs-shouldnt-eat-but-do/*.

"The Trail Sled Dog Race." *Iditarod, www.iditarod.com/*.

"2000 Yukon Quest: World's Strongest Dog Team." *Everything Husky*, *www.everythinghusky.com/features/questpull2000.htm*.

"Vocalizations." *Natural History Museum of Los Angeles County*, *www.nhm.org/exhibitions/dogs/communication/vocalizations.html*.

Walsh, Diana and Stacy Finz. "The Peterson Trial." *San Francisco Chronicle*, September 1, 2004, *www.sfgate.com/cgi-bin/article.cgi?f=/c/a/2004/09/01/BAG1U8HJIE17.DTL*.

Walton, Marsha. "Dog breed works hand-in-paw with owners." *CNN*, October 17, 2003, *www.cnn.com/2003/TECH/science/10/16/coolsc.Bordercollies/index.html*.

Willing, Richard. "Court Looks at Dogs, Drugs, Privacy." *USA Today*, November 10, 2004.

Wollard, Kathy. "How Come: Lucky dogs can hear what we can't." *Newsday*, June 9, 2008.

"Wonder Dog Climbs Trees in Pursuit of Birds." *Truveo*, *www. truveo.com/Wonder-Dog-Climbs-Trees-In-Pursuit-Of-Birds/id/3772992830*.

Yeon, Seong Chan. "The Vocal Communication of Canines." *Journal of Veterinary Behavior*, 2007 (2).

Yin, Sophia, "A New Perspective on Barking in Dogs." *Journal of Comparative Psychology*, 2002, Vol. 16.

Yin, Sophia, and Brenda McCowan. "Barking in Domestic Dogs: Context Specificity and Individual Identification." *Animal Behaviour. Davis, Calif.: University of California Davis, 2004.*

Your dog will kiss you on the chops,

if you review our book.
on your favorite online
retail website

Made in the USA
Columbia, SC
16 December 2018